Soul Space

Formerly employed in the computer industry, and trained by the Jesuits in accompanying others in prayer, Margaret Silf is now engaged full-time in writing, facilitating retreats and days of reflection and as a companion to others on their spiritual journeying. Born and brought up in Yorkshire, Margaret now lives in Staffordshire, and is married with one daughter. She is an ecumenical Christian, committed to working across and beyond the denominational boundaries.

She is the author of *Daysprings: Daily Readings for a Life with God*; *Landmarks: An Ignatian Journey*; *The Miller's Tale and Other Parables*; *Taste and See: Adventuring Into Prayer*; *Wayfaring: A Gospel Journey Into Life* (all Darton, Longman and Todd), and *Sacred Spaces: Stations on a Celtic Way* (Lion Publishing).

Soul Space
Making a Retreat in the
Christian Tradition

Margaret Silf

Published in Great Britain in 2002

Society for Promoting Christian Knowledge
36 Causton Street
London SW1P 4ST

British Library Cataloguing-in-Publication Data
A catalogue record for this book is available from the British Library

ISBN 0-281-05317-0

[3 5 7 9 10 8 6 4 2]

Typeset by David Gregson Associates, Beccles
Printed in Great Britain by
The Cromwell Press, Trowbridge

Contents

CONTENTS

Why retreat?

There's something about the word 'retreat' that can either set our hearts leaping at the prospect, or make us run a mile from the very idea of making one. For some people the word resonates with memories of school retreats, that they either loved or hated. For others it sounds like something only nuns and priests would ever think of doing. Or it can be a word that touches into deep longings for the possibility of space, time and solitude. For almost everyone, the thought of making a retreat for the first time is a daunting one. The possibility raises a whole range of questions, from 'What will it be like?' right through to 'How do I know I won't be brain-washed?' A little solid knowledge of what retreats are all about and how they work can go a long way in encouraging us to step over the brink of making a retreat. Which is why SPCK invited me to explore the process a little in this book, in the hope of addressing some of those questions and shedding light on some of the many different types of retreat and what can be expected of them.

It is probably true to say that in some way, most of us make a retreat, most of the days of our lives. A harassed mother slips off to the bathroom, and just sits there in uninterrupted peace for five minutes, behind a locked door. An exhausted bus driver takes the dog for an evening walk in the park. A child hides away in a secret den in the loft, to be alone for a while where her siblings can't find her, while she mulls over her feelings about a problem at school. All of them little retreats, and from this deep instinctive need for space and peace, we can begin to notice what actually makes a 'retreat', and what we are looking for when we make one.

What makes a retreat?

What are the main qualities that turn ordinary time into *graced* time, with the power to renew, to challenge, and to redirect us? The following features may give us a clue:

- Time in retreat is 'time apart'. For a short period, we withdraw from our routine activity. We may do this by physically going to a different place, or we may make a definite change to the environment where we spend our time day by day, creating 'space for the soul' wherever we happen to be.
- During our time apart we enjoy a stillness, in contrast to the normal 'noise' of our daily activity. We may begin by switching off the external sounds of radio or TV, but with practice we will also learn the art of switching off the constant noise that tends to go on in our own heads. We become physically still, but we also cease our constant inner 'busyness' for a while. In this deeper stillness, we begin to glimpse what is happening at the ground of our being – the heart of ourselves, where our deepest feelings and highest visions start to show themselves.
- In these times of quiet, our *focus* changes. Gradually, as we relax our bodies, we also begin to relax our hold on the personal anxieties of the day, and there is room for the wider world. Perspective lengthens, as we come to stillness. We see ourselves as parts of a greater whole, and there is strength and peace in that reassurance.
- This larger perspective leads us back to the demands of everyday life, but with a more balanced view. We have dipped into a deeper layer of our own psyche, and sometimes we will find solutions and new directions that escape us while we are living in the cut and thrust of the daily struggle to survive.

A retreat is always a spiritual experience, whether or not the person making it would call themselves 'spiritual'. It always takes us closer to the core of our being – a space where we also touch the reality of God.

Retreating from *or retreating* for?

Sadly, many of us will have taken on board some variation of the classic criticism: 'Stop dreaming and get on with something useful.' Parents all too easily derail their children's natural instinct to seek time and space simply to 'be'. Children, perhaps, counter this attack on their inner world by using the gift of play. In play we can 'be'. The pressure to 'do' is suspended, while we simply enjoy activities that are not intended to produce or achieve anything. As we grow older, however, we lose much of our playfulness, and we begin to feel guilty if we are not occupying our every moment with something that will produce some tangible result.

Not surprising, therefore, that we begin to question our motives as adults, if we feel we would like to make a retreat. We may wonder whether we are in fact just looking for an escape route from the demands of our normal life. And if we don't question this for ourselves, there will probably be others who will. This may account for some of the awkwardness about wanting to take time out to go deeper into what our living is really about. Are we running away from our problems, or are we turning our hearts in the direction of new solutions? Why do so many people who make a retreat avoid telling their work colleagues where they are going and why? Why do individuals often step back from making a retreat for fear of what the family will say? When we 'retreat', is it really just an escape?

Perhaps a return to reflect on those many little 'retreats' we make, almost without noticing, in the course of our daily lives, will lead us to some answers. Initially, it is true, these brief withdrawals from the daily routine are a reaction to pressure. We withdraw *from* the routine, seeking a space for stillness. But once that stillness is discovered, we find that there is a treasure enfolded in it that is indeed worth retreating *for*.

Perhaps we could call that 'treasure' the deepened perspective we gain, or the new balance we find, which enables us to return to daily life more creatively. There is also a new focus, beyond 'self' to 'other'. The brief withdrawal may help us to recognize a way of coping with the difficult colleague, or more effective ways of expressing our feelings to our families, or a practical way of engaging with the struggle to shape a more just society. These small, but very significant, changes of view and attitude are typical of what happens in a retreat, whether that retreat is a sustained period of silence in a retreat house, or just a few minutes of quiet reflection in a busy day.

The quest for 'enlightenment'

As scripture records, Jesus frequently 'retreated' to be alone with his Father in the core of his being. At times of major decision, he did so for extended periods of time, discerning his way forward in the silence of the hills. This model alone should be enough to encourage us, who bear his name, to follow his example.

And the mystics, of all faith traditions and of none, have always engaged in what we might call the quest for enlightenment. It all sounds rather pompous and 'out-of-this-world', and not very relevant to us, who have to live our lives very solidly *in* this world. Yet 'enlightenment' is what wakes us all up every morning, as the sun rises. 'Enlightenment' is what enables us to see where we are going and what we are about and gives us the invisible energy to get on with our living.

I met this kind of everyday 'enlightenment' in a particularly vivid way one morning while on holiday on an island in the Mediterranean. It was about 6 a.m. but time wasn't important. I was on holiday. My watch was set aside, buried under all the unnecessary 'necessities' I had thought I would need. And the absence of my watch seemed to make me more aware of the natural rhythms of the day. The rising sun – with its power to penetrate sleep with a determination stronger than my natural laziness. The noonday sun, compelling siesta. The lengthening shadows of evening, setting the night music going and releasing a cooler energy. And the non-negotiable dark of a near-desert night, pouring an infusion of silence into the cocktail of life.

It reminded me of how my awareness of time changes during a retreat, and how healing and restoring it can be to exchange the time-tabled world for the natural cycles of dawn, day, dusk and darkness.

And so I began to look forward each morning to the moment when the tiniest gleam of gold appeared at the summit of the hills beyond my bedroom window. As if some divine finger had struck a match-head and created light and fire for all the ages still to come. And then, ever so gradually, flowing down the hillside, flooding the valley, a tide of daylight, bringing a whole new day to life.

It seems to me that humankind must always have gazed with the same sense of breath-held wonder as new light dawned. In every culture, through all ages, in all tongues, through the infinite variety of fable, the story of the coming of light is told and retold. A daily miracle, a perennial focus for the human quest for all that lies beyond itself.

As I remember this Mediterranean sunrise, I can think of no simpler, nor any more potent expression of enlightenment than this – to greet the dawn with an expectant awareness, and to let its life-giving energy tumble through every crevasse of life on earth.

In a retreat, whatever form it may take, we are seeking something of this enlightenment in our own living. We climb, symbolically, to a hilltop place, by stepping aside for a while from our everyday concerns, to allow God to dawn anew in us, illuminating the deeper recesses of our minds and hearts and to let his presence flow on, from that encounter into the plains and valleys of our everyday lives.

But 'enlightenment' doesn't, of course, depend on remote mountain tops and Mediterranean dawns. Nor does it depend on our being able to take time out from our normal routine in any complicated or expensive way, to reflect on the ways in which God's energy may be active in our living. I hope that this book will open up some possibilities of stepping aside, however briefly, to make time for God, in ways that, perhaps, you may not have considered before.

'Enlightenment' happens every time we draw back the bedroom curtains and look out upon a new day. It happens, in fact, whenever we take a moment to gaze at the world as if seeing it with God's eyes. This can take us by surprise many times in the course of a single day. When we watch a sleeping child, for example, or notice the steady breathing of a loved one, when we see how the cobwebs on the downspout have turned to lace under the touch of frost, or notice one drop of dew on a rose petal. All these are moments of 'retreat'. They are all visits to our 'soul space' – that inner space in the depths of our hearts, where God is at home. These moments, like my early morning meeting with the sunrise, can suggest to us something of the nature of what it is to enter into 'retreat':

- They happen when we go 'out of ourselves' and let creation speak its own language to our hearts. We cannot manufacture them. We can only experience them.
- They take us 'out of time'. We enter, as it were, an invisible world where time ceases to drive us.
- They flow with their own natural rhythms, and they draw us, like-wise, into those rhythms, that we may well feel we have completely lost under the pressures of competitive living.
- They energize us. We might find it hard to describe just how this energizing happens, but we can feel its effects. We come away from our times in our 'soul space' with a renewed vitality and, perhaps, a deeper insight into the heart of things. The 'tide of day-light' that I watched coursing down the hillside while on holiday is a picture of the kind of energy that God releases in us when we take time to be still with him. It too brings a 'whole new day' to life in us. It flows right down into the valleys of our lives, changing the way we see things, making new things possible, opening up new pathways and views.

All these are features of a 'retreat', whether it takes just half an hour of stillness in a quiet spot, or lasts for days or even months in the cloistered silence of a retreat house. Ordinary time is suspended, to make a little space for eternity to reveal itself. The rhythm of our living begins to align itself with the natural rhythms of light and darkness, activity and rest. And in ways we need not understand, we find new energy in the process, and return to our routine enabled to live from a greater depth than before.

The purpose of this book is to open up some of the ways in which we can help this to happen. It suggests some ways of taking 'time out' to experience the deeper sources of our being. These include the traditional ways of making a retreat in a secluded environment, and the increasingly accessible ways of entering 'soul space' within the routine of our daily lives. All are ways of being at the oasis, and of going to the well of living water that is always there for us, if we can 'pause' the video of our 'busy-ness' long enough to draw from it.

Using this book

If you are feeling drawn to the idea of making a retreat, I hope that this book will encourage you in a number of ways:

- By helping you to find a way of making a retreat that suits your personal circumstances. In Part I the book looks at some of the circumstances surrounding different people and lifestyles and offers suggestions as to what kind of retreat might be appropriate. You may find it helpful to browse through the different 'profiles' outlined, and reflect on whether any of the suggestions appeals to you. Each of these 'profiles' cross-refers (using a bold typeface) to related entries in the Fact File in Part IV that provide more detail about a particular type of retreat or aspect of retreat-making.
- By attempting to address some of the questions most commonly raised about retreats and offering honest answers. Part II looks at 'the questions you didn't like to ask'.
- By suggesting, in Part III, some ways of preparing for a period of retreat, making the most of it while you are in it, and of sustaining the experience after your return to daily life.
- By providing a guide to what you can expect to happen in different types of retreat, and what is meant by some of the terms used in the world of retreat-making. Part IV takes the form of a Fact File, comprising a number of entries, arranged in alphabetical order. These entries are cross-referenced from other parts of the book, by the use of a bold typeface.
- By offering some first-hand accounts of different types of retreat in Part V.

The book looks at ways of discovering 'soul space', whether you have only half a day to spare, or are able to go into seclusion for weeks at a time. It suggests ways of making a retreat without breaking the bank or demolishing family harmony, and describes the traditional retreat opportunities in retreat houses.

Whatever kind of retreat you are looking for, you will find an invaluable friend and ally in the Retreat Association, whose address is given at the end of the book. This association produces a listing each year of all the main retreat opportunities in the United Kingdom and describes the facilities offered. This listings magazine, called simply *Retreats*, appears every autumn and is available at most Christian bookshops or direct from the Retreat Association, whose staff are also happy to offer personal advice by phone.

A word of thanks . . .

. . . to so many people who have helped in the shaping of this book.

My special thanks go to Kerry Hiscock for her invaluable insights, searching questions and comments and her tireless patience in reading and rereading the draft; to Paddy Lane of the Retreat Association for all her support and encouragement and the information and advice she has so generously provided; to Breda Gainey, Gerry Hughes and Michael Ivens for their generosity in taking time to read and comment on the draft; to those who so kindly contributed the first-hand accounts in Part V: Ann Ashton, Teresa Booth, Breda Gainey, Mary Griffiths, Kerry Hiscock, Beverley Hollins, Dorothy Millichamp, Rosemary Millward and Deborah Oram; and to my colleagues at SPCK, especially Liz Marsh for inviting me to write the book and encouraging me all along the way, and Claire Sauer for her valued editorial work.

It is impossible to give due thanks to the many, many people who contribute to the wealth of retreat opportunities now available. However, my special personal thanks go to my Jesuit friends Gerry Hughes and Michael Ivens (who have pioneered the growth of Ignatian retreats in the UK, and made them accessible to lay people, and in daily life), Fintan Creavan, Brian McClorry, Damian Jackson, Tom McGuinness and Paul Nicholson, all who work alongside them and all who have accompanied my own retreats.

To all who have sown the seeds of prayer in our time and place, we who reap the fruits thank you, and thank God.

Part I
Beginning Where You Are

This section describes a few specific situations, reflecting different needs and hopes for discovering 'soul space' in retreat, ranging from the desire to 'try it out', maybe for just a day or a weekend, and see how it suits you, through to the desire to go into deep seclusion for a much longer period. Find the 'profile' that most closely resembles your own aspirations, and use it as a pointer to the type of retreat that might best fulfil your needs.

Cross-references to entries in Part IV are printed in bold type.

Confined to your own four walls?

In a culture which values 'freedom' so highly, it is quite amazing how many of us are, in effect, prisoners of our personal circumstances. Sometimes this sense of being trapped in our own little world is a mere inconvenience. Sometimes it feels like a dead weight upon our lives.

Take, for example, the situation of a single parent, at home with small children under school age. 'Going out' for such a person, means taking the children to school, or trawling them round the supermarket. Occasionally there might be an hour with a friend over coffee, while they jointly supervise the little ones. Adult companionship, and time 'just to be' are at a premium.

These circumstances are paralleled by many similar stories of virtual 'house arrest'. The following are a few examples:

- People who are caring for sick or elderly relatives.
- People who are sick or convalescing and are unable to go out independently.
- People who, for whatever reason, are afraid to venture out alone.
- People who are trying to 'grow' spiritually, but are faced with opposition or even an outright veto from their partner or immediate family.

Retreats in daily life

The hope of a 'retreat' for such people is a cruel dream. But does it have to be so? Over recent years the popularity of retreats has grown tremendously. Many more people have heard of the possibility of making a retreat, but by the same token, many people have felt this to be an impossible dream for one or more of the reasons mentioned above. Necessity has proved to be the mother of invention, and much thought has been given to the challenge of opening up the 'retreat experience' to those many people who cannot leave home for any length of time, for either personal or financial reasons.

A **retreat in daily life** is an opportunity to set aside a special time of either a week, or perhaps several weeks, during which you undertake to give time to prayer each day, and to meet with an experienced companion, commonly called a **prayer companion/prayer guide**, either daily for about half an hour (in a one-week intensive retreat) or once or twice a week during a longer, more spaced-out retreat. Apart from the time set aside for prayer, and the time to talk with your companion, your daily routine continues unchanged. The cost of such a retreat is minimal, usually amounting only to the cost of defraying any travel expenses of the prayer companions. In some cases, if you are housebound, the companion will be able to visit you in your own home.

In any form of daily life retreat, your retreat companion will suggest a focus for your prayer during the time between meetings. He or she will simply *accompany* you. There will be no attempt to persuade you along paths you do not choose, or to influence you in any way. You are the pilgrim, choosing for yourself how you will make the journey. The companion will simply listen and reflect back to you anything you have shared that sheds light on the way your journey is evolving.

Retreats in daily life are often centred on local parishes or church communities, but are increasingly being arranged in workplaces or centres of study. If you belong to a church, you might approach your priest or minister in the first instance to ask whether any facilities exist in your area for making a daily life retreat. If not, you might be able to persuade him or her to think about arranging one. Otherwise, try making contact with representatives of one of the growing number of **spirituality networks** (see addresses at the end of the book), who should be able to put you in touch with local opportunities.

'Open door' retreats

The Cenacle Sisters, faced with the challenge of offering 'sacred space' to people in these confining situations, refused to take 'No!' for an answer, and have developed their special vision of 'open door retreats'. An **open door retreat** is a more structured form of retreat in daily life, and can also be organized locally so that participants only need to make arrangements to get to a local meeting point for short gatherings over a period of a few weeks. These are

faith sharing meetings offering an opportunity to explore the most important questions of your inner journey, with a companion who will listen to your story, and help you to discern where God has been active in your life, and where you feel he is leading you now.

This experience is based on the principles of St Ignatius Loyola, whose insights have shaped the way in which many **individually given retreats** are conducted. Your companion will have been trained specifically in the giving of open door retreats, and will offer you space to explore your own issues within a framework of scriptural reflections and personal prayer.

The retreat will normally extend over nine weeks, and when it is over you will almost certainly find that you are in touch with a wider network of fellow pilgrims than you would have thought possible when you first set out. For many people an open door retreat has become the start of a new, and radically less lonely, way of making the journey of life with God.

Retreats 'behind closed doors'

If you are unfortunate enough to find yourself behind closed doors in a more radical way, this needn't mean that a retreat is impossible. Increasingly, local spirituality networks are offering retreats in daily life in HM prisons. In this situation the retreat guides arrange to visit the prison at regular intervals, and conduct one-to-one meetings with each retreatant, just as in a standard retreat in daily life.

If you are interested in making a retreat in these circumstances, speak to your prison chaplain in the first instance, or contact Christian friends outside the prison to see if you can find any information on local networks who might be willing to approach the prison authorities to initiate a retreat.

Faith sharing groups can also be established in a prison environment.

The Spiritual Exercises in daily life

To make the full Exercises of St Ignatius Loyola is a big commitment, but an immensely fruitful undertaking if you are prepared to make a sustained journey of prayer over several months. St Ignatius himself envisaged the possibility that a potential retreatant might not be able to withdraw from daily duties for weeks at a time, and he suggested (and indeed used) an adaptation of his Spiritual Exercises to be made over a period of about nine months within the context of daily life and work. This form of making the Exercises is known as the 'Nineteenth Annotation' because it is described in the nineteenth of a set of additional notes that Ignatius includes in his text of the Exercises.

The form of the Exercises is described more fully in Part IV (see **Spiritual Exercises of St Ignatius**, and **Spiritual Exercises in daily life**). The Nineteenth Annotation requires a time of prayer each day (usually about an hour) and a meeting every two weeks or so with an experienced companion who guides the retreatant through a structured programme of scriptural meditations, but it does not require the retreatant to leave his or her normal routine, and it is considerably cheaper than making the full Exercises residentially in a retreat house.

Ongoing spiritual companionship

If the idea of making a structured retreat, following a specific programme, does not appeal to you, but you are looking for individual spiritual companionship or **soul friendship**, the Retreat Association will be happy to put you in touch with someone in your area who would welcome a chance to share the journey with you, and who is experienced in accompanying others in prayer and spiritual exploration. The Retreat Association will give you the name of a local contact person, who will in turn be in touch with a network of fellow pilgrims. You are then quite free to follow up any suggested contacts or not, as you wish.

Spirituality networks

There are also a number of so-called **spirituality networks** around the country and overseas. These are groupings of people seeking to follow a similar kind of spiritual journey. The networks are nothing more, essentially, than a link of people in a particular area who know about each other, and who may meet together from time to time to share ideas and inspiration. Usually someone among them will be responsible for keeping an up-to-date list of contact names and addresses. Depending on the type of grouping, some networks will follow a fairly structured approach in their meetings, while others will impose no structure at all.

Examples of such networks include:

- The Ignatian spirituality networks in the main regions of the UK (see Contacts section). These networks enable people who are drawn to the Ignatian way to be in contact with each other. Some of them offer basic training in listening skills and accompanying others in prayer, for those who wish it, and they all offer daily life retreats, on request, to people in their regions.
- The **Christian Life Community** (CLC), also based on the spirituality of St Ignatius. This international organization comprises a widespread network of small groups of between 2 and 12 or so people who meet regularly to share their experience of spiritual journeying. Each group is free to decide for itself how to structure its meetings and what material to use as a focus, but excellent material and guidelines are provided by the umbrella organization for those who wish to use it. The CLC is Jesuit-inspired, and each region has the benefit of a Jesuit chaplain. It is ecumenical and welcomes all who are seeking to deepen their life in God and feel drawn to an Ignatian path.
- The 'Third Order' organizations, or groupings of people who feel drawn towards a particular spirituality (for example, the Carmelite way or the Franciscan way), and would like to be actively associated with the parent religious order, without actually entering religious life. Associates or 'third order' members agree to live an appropriate lifestyle, and usually take a form of vow, but they pursue their membership of the order within their normal daily life, family and work settings. They have regular meetings together for prayer and to encourage and nourish growth in their chosen way.
- **Julian Meetings**, silent prayer groups, whose spirituality is inspired by Dame Julian of Norwich. Julian groups meet regularly in circles of silent contemplative prayer. A Julian Meeting usually comprises a group of between 6 and 15 people who gather in a private house, church or chapel. More details about the nature of

the groups and their meetings, and of other opportunities for joining in silent prayer, are included in Part IV. If you are looking for a regular oasis of silent prayer, with like-minded people, a Julian Meeting or other silent prayer group might be the place to search.

Lonely, but computer-literate?

If you are 'confined to barracks', or even tied to a workstation in the office with no other colleagues who would be 'on your wavelength' spiritually, you might like to log into the web site called 'Sacred Space' on

http://www.jesuit.ie/prayer

This site has been developed by the Irish Jesuits, and provides an excellent and refreshingly accessible approach to daily meditation. Information on the screen guides you through a daily reflection, allowing you plenty of space to explore your own experience as you go.

Perhaps you are 'home alone', or seizing a few precious minutes while the baby is asleep or the children are watching TV. Or maybe you are feeling trapped at your office desk, envying those who have 'time to pray'. Wherever you find yourself, if you have internet access you will find this web site a marvellous companion for your journey. The site is changed regularly and offers new suggestions and fresh insights every day, which can be used in privacy at whatever time suits you.

Explore the Internet, too, for links with other spiritual pilgrims seeking email contact. As always, however, with random Internet connections, take care when 'corresponding' with strangers, especially on matters as deep and significant as your journey with God.

The Tablet and other Christian periodicals often include reviews of interesting web sites you might like to explore.

A video experience

Another way of deepening your prayer in isolation might be to use a video course. There are many stimulating offerings on the market, as a browse round any good religious booksellers will reveal. An excellent example of such a series is the video marketed jointly by the BBC and the Bible Society, called *Tales from the Madhouse*, which is a reissue of a series of eight programmes televised during the Easter season and now available for individual and group use. Each of the eight 15-minute dramatizations looks in depth at one of the characters associated with the events of the first Eastertide, but in a challenging and engaging way which goes well beyond the scriptural accounts. The video is accompanied by notes and suggestions for group discussion and individual or group meditation.

Home-based groups

You may find that in time you can break out of your isolation, perhaps by inviting friends to share something of their spiritual journey, in your own home. **Faith sharing meetings** of this kind can become a much cherished 'retreat time' for all concerned, and for many this kind of private networking is a lifeline.

To create genuine retreat time in your own home, make sure that all members of the group agree the ground rules for the sharing of their experience. It is wise to make such a group strictly a 'listening' group. This means that each person has an opportunity to share whatever he or she feels comfortable in sharing, and is assured of respectful silence. It can be helpful to light a candle, or create some other focus upon which people can centre themselves. There should be no discussion, much less any argument, arising from what is shared, and there should be no attempt to 'correct' other people's views or resolve their problems. This is a sharing forum, not a therapy session. Discussion groups, prayer groups, and Bible study groups are, of course, all very valuable encounters, but they lie beyond the scope of this book, and are not the same thing as sharing sacred space in quiet, non-judgemental acceptance. Many people discover the gift of being genuinely and lovingly listened to for the first time in such a group. This is what makes a home group into a retreat space.

Self-directed retreats

Another response to the growing demand for retreat opportunities has come in the form of books that offer readers a programmed journey of prayer that can be undertaken in their own home and at their own pace. A book of this nature will, typically, suggest a theme or focus for your day's prayer, supported by scriptural texts and sometimes other material such as poems or suggestions for practical activities.

Some of these books offer excellent guidance on making a home-based retreat, and a few are listed in the suggestions for further reading at the back of this book. You will benefit most from such a retreat, however, if you also have a companion with whom you can reflect on how the prayer has been for you and where you feel God is acting in your life.

If you are doubtful as to whether a sustained retreat (either in daily life or in a retreat house) would be the right thing for you, you might find that using one of these books for a week or so would help you discern whether a focused period of guided prayer would be helpful to you at this stage of your life.

Unsure about the whole idea?

The decision to make a retreat can be a big, and perhaps a daunting, step. All kinds of questions arise, some of which are addressed in Part II. What will be expected of me? Will I be able to cope with silence? Will I be able to pray? And many more.

A good plan, if you have never made a retreat before, is to take things gently, and dip your toe in the water before you take the plunge. If you are feeling apprehensive about making a retreat over several days, you are not alone! And because so many people are now looking for opportunities to make a retreat, new possibilities are emerging to help you feel your way in and discover in a non-threatening way just what might be helpful to you and what will not.

Quiet days

Before you commit yourself to a longer retreat, why not try a quiet day? Many of the retreat centres listed in *Retreats* offer **quiet days** as a regular feature of their programmes. These days will normally be led by someone experienced in retreat giving, who will share some thoughts on an aspect of the 'inner journey' or the practice of prayer and reflection. The purpose of this input is not to offer a 'course of instruction', but to suggest some ways of focusing your thoughts and going deeper into the stillness where you are touching the ground of your being and the dwelling place of God within you. If the input isn't helpful to you personally, then leave it aside and follow the promptings of your own heart. Nothing is compulsory during a day of retreat like this.

As well as introducing the theme of the day, the leader may make him or herself available to anyone who would like to talk privately.

The main part of the day will offer time simply to be still, to pray, to reflect, to ponder, to *be*. Usually there will be ample space for people to spread out through the house and find a congenial spot to be alone and at peace. You can use the time in any way you choose, provided that you allow others their space and their silence.

The day may well include a period of shared prayer or worship, and possibly a more formal service, perhaps with communion. Again, you are free to attend or not, as you wish.

Drop-in days

A drop-in day is a less formal form of quiet day. Many retreat centres give an open invitation to people simply to 'drop in', as the name suggests, for as long as they wish, on designated days. If you are looking for an oasis of calm, you will find it in such a centre, and no one will bother you or ask you what you are up to. You will be left to find your own space if this is what you want. However, if you want to talk to someone, this is usually possible on request. There are a growing number of 'drop-in centres' in our towns and cities, where people come to find an hour or so of restful reflection amid the shopping or after work. 'Droppers in' are usually welcome to join in any of the prayer or worship that may be going on in the centre at the time.

Increasingly, churches, especially those within the Free Church tradition, are opening up their premises as drop-in centres to be used as quiet space for those seeking time and space to be still in the midst of daily life. Look out for opportunities like this as you move around, and also as detailed in the listings in *Retreats*.

Quiet gardens

In recent years the Quiet Garden Movement has evolved, as a network of opportunities for enjoying the peace and contemplative silence of a beautiful garden. **Quiet gardens** come into existence when someone agrees to open their own garden for occasional days of stillness and reflection. The Quiet Garden Trust initiates and supports this vision and will supply a list of gardens in this country and worldwide that offer this kind of hospitality.

The vision of the Quiet Garden Trust is to open up gardens of prayer where visitors may experience silence and solitude, while appreciating the natural beauty of the garden and perhaps learning a little more about the possibilities of contemplative prayer.

A typical day of reflection in a quiet garden begins with some time (perhaps 30 to 45 minutes) of teaching or the presentation of a theme, followed by tea or coffee. The second part of the morning is available for quiet prayer or activity, such as reading, walking, drawing, writing, or simply being still. There may be a period of simple prayer at midday, followed by a 'bring and share' lunch.

The afternoon offers time to rest or reflect again in silence and ends with evening prayer, a cup of tea and a chance to talk with the other participants. There will usually be someone available to listen, during the day, if you would like to talk one-to-one.

Retreats on the streets

For many people, especially those who are active in the cause of justice and peace, the idea of a quiet day 'away from it all' can sound 'escapist' (although I hope that this book will convince you that this is not the case). A retreat can be a very active undertaking, and a way of making a radical identification with the marginalized people in our town and cities.

In some towns it is possible to make a 'retreat on the streets'. This involves a day living on the streets and seeking to engage with the real needs and feelings of those who are living there not by choice but of necessity.

This kind of retreat can take many forms, but a typical day might begin with shared prayer and ecumenical worship and a simple shared breakfast, after which the participants go off into the city, with a very small sum of money (typically less than £1), to fend for themselves through the day, and to seek to become more deeply aware of how it feels to be on the streets with less than the cost of a simple meal in your pocket. The participants are free to shape the day in their own way, but may well take the opportunity to talk with those they meet who are homeless, unemployed, disturbed or addicted. While this offers only a glimpse of the stark reality of street life, it is nevertheless a deeply moving and challenging experience for those who undertake it.

The day often ends with a chance to gather again with the other participants and share the insights and feelings of the day. This often leads to new initiatives for relieving the suffering that has been witnessed.

'Away weekends'

For many people the weekend is the only time they can, realistically, take time out for themselves without sabotaging the family holiday.

The possibilities for making a short weekend retreat are almost infinite. A glance through the pages of *Retreats* will reveal some of the experiences on offer. These range from a theme weekend to a time of silence alone in a monastic community.

A **theme retreat** weekend offers you the opportunity to go away from Friday evening to Sunday afternoon, enjoying two nights and two days in a retreat centre, with full board. These weekends fall into three main categories:

- Weekends to focus on a particular topic or aspect of the inner journey; for example, 'Celtic Spirituality' or 'Finding God's Will', or aspects of the struggle for justice and peace.
- Weekends for a particular group of people, offering them space to explore their own needs and feelings in a safe environment. Examples include weekends for the bereaved, for the divorced or for gay people. Some centres also offer weekends especially for those with special needs; for example, weekends for the deaf, conducted in sign language.
- Weekends in which to pursue a particular activity with like-minded people; these include weekends for painting, embroidery,

calligraphy, circle dancing and many more. These activities can also be pursued in a prayerful setting over a longer period, of course.

If you are looking rather for two days of space and silence, with no instruction or interaction with other retreatants, you might prefer to find a monastic centre, many of which welcome weekend or short-term visitors to enjoy their hospitality and join in their community prayer if they so wish. A weekend like this would be unstructured, apart from the daily offices and you would be free to shape it to your own needs entirely, though again there would almost certainly be someone available to listen, if you wished to talk one-to-one.

'First time retreats'

A number of retreat houses now offer what they call '**first time retreats**'. These are usually shorter than the traditional six or eight days, and they provide more help in exploring new forms of prayer, for example, or on how to structure your day in a way that will help you get the most out of your retreat. If the retreat is basically a silent one, you will probably find in a 'first time retreat' that the silence is not so absolute. There may be more opportunity for verbal interaction with the retreat leaders, and even with the other participants. You will have the chance to experience the deep silence of a retreat, but possibly only for a few hours at a time.

The *Retreats* magazine gives details of many of the first time retreats being offered in any year. If this is what you are looking for, just browse *Retreats* and see what appeals to you. If you would like to know more about a particular retreat, don't hesitate to phone the retreat centre and ask. They are there to help you, and they will welcome your enquiry.

A typical day in a first time retreat will be similar to that described under **individually given retreats** in Part IV, except that it will also include some instruction on an aspect of the journey of prayer, or on new approaches to prayer that you might like to try. It may include guidance on using art or clay to help you in your prayer, and maybe also the opportunity to share your experience with a small group of other retreatants.

DIY weekends and quiet days

If you are involved with any kind of faith sharing group or spirituality network, you will almost certainly want to arrange quiet days
or weekends for yourselves. You will find, in *Retreats*, the details
of retreat centres who will welcome you to use their facilities but
arrange your own weekend in your own way. Usually the retreat
centre will ask for only a modest donation to cover costs. They
will almost always be able to offer tea and coffee, and a place for
you to enjoy your 'bring and share' lunch, or they may offer soup
and sandwiches or a full lunch by arrangement.

It is a good idea for a member of the group to visit the centre beforehand to check the parking arrangements and the accommodation,
and establish a rapport with the centre leaders.

And if you have enjoyed a quiet day yourself, there is nothing to
stop you offering a day in your own home or garden.

Longing for space and silence?

I remember meeting someone on a quiet day once in a retreat centre
in northern England. During the course of the afternoon she told
me that this was the first time in over 20 years that she had been
able to spend as much as a single hour alone in silence. For all
those years she had always been surrounded by the clamour of
husband and children or work colleagues, and she found herself in
heaven when at last the quiet day gave her space just to stand still
and observe something of the shape and focus of her life.

Today, perhaps more than ever before, many, many people long
for such space, and surprising numbers of them rarely, if ever,
manage to get it. You might like to reflect for a moment on what
those words mean to you? Space. Solitude. Silence. If there is a
voice in your depths crying out for just that, then you will probably
be contemplating the possibility of making a rather longer retreat,
away from home and work, in a retreat centre or monastic house
somewhere. If this is your desire, there are still several possibilities.
The following questions might help to identify what would best
suit your needs:

- Would you like to have a companion or guide to talk with for a while each day to share how your prayer is going? Or would you rather be left completely alone?
- Do you want to cater for yourself, or would you like the retreat house to provide all you need?
- Do you prefer simplicity, or is it important to you to have warmth, comfort and privacy?
- Do you want to be alone, or do you value being part of a group of people journeying together, even in the silence?

The main options for a silent, sustained retreat can be summarized as:

- An **individually given retreat** also called an individually guided retreat, and often abbreviated to IGR.
- A period of retreat in a religious house or retreat centre with no personal guidance.
- A period of retreat alone, wherever you feel drawn to be.

The first two options can be either full-board or self-catering, depending on the retreat centre you choose. For the third option, self-catering will be the norm.

What happens during an individually given retreat?

So you have decided to take the plunge and sign up for a longer retreat, usually either six or eight days. What have you let yourself in for?

A week is a long time to spend in prayer. You will probably want to spend some time in preparation, and some guidelines for this are given in Part III. So let us suppose the day has arrived, and you are on your way to your chosen retreat house.

Most retreat houses encourage retreatants to arrive around mid-afternoon, to give them time to settle in before the retreat proper begins in the evening. When you arrive you will be *welcomed*. You will probably find that this is the kind of welcome you would receive when visiting a friend's house, rather than the cool courtesy of a hotel reception. A member of the retreat team, or one of the household will meet you, greet you, and show you your room. You will probably be invited to relax with a cup of tea, and maybe shown around the house. It can feel like the first day at 'big school' and you may fear that you will never find your room again if once you leave it. Be reassured: after the first day you will be feeling at home, and nobody will ever mind you asking for help if you need anything at all.

In your room, or on a notice board, you will find the timetable of the house, and any other information you need to feel comfortable and at ease. The timetable, for a guided retreat, will usually consist of nothing more complicated than the mealtimes and the times of any shared worship. The rest of the day is yours to do as you like in. Remember that absolutely everything is optional. When you entered the door of the retreat house, you did not take permanent vows! You are here to meet God in your own way, and the routine of the house is there to help you do this. You are free to come and go as you wish, and to join in worship as and when you wish. All that might be asked is that you sign a list one day in advance to let the kitchen staff know if you are going to miss a main meal, so that unnecessary food wastage is avoided. In some retreat houses you may also be asked to take a share, usually only on one day, in clearing up after the main meals. This helps to keep running costs down, and is a small way of ministering to your fellow retreatants. And if you enjoy some physical activity, the retreat house will probably not say 'No' to some help with the garden if you should feel so inclined.

On the first evening of your retreat, if you are one of a group making the retreat at the same time, there will probably be an opportunity for you to gather together, before the silence begins. This is a chance to get to know each other a little, and also to meet the people who will be accompanying you. Typically one **retreat guide (or retreat director)** may be accompanying five or six retreatants during the week, and often your guide will arrange a short meeting for the five or six of you on the first evening. Sometimes this meeting will include a time of quiet prayer together, or a chance to introduce yourselves, and to arrange the times for the daily meetings between the guide and the retreatants. If this is your first retreat, your guide will be especially aware of making sure that you feel at ease. If anything at all comes up during the week, whether deeply spiritual or completely practical, your guide is the first point of contact. He or she is there to make sure that any problems are sorted out, and that your quiet is undisturbed as far as is humanly possible.

At this point it is perhaps important to mention that your guide will also have a 'supervisor', and will meet with that person regularly, to share anything that has come up for him or her in the course of listening to the sharing of the retreatants. This **supervision** meeting, between your guide and his or her supervisor is strictly about the agenda of your guide, and under no circumstances will a guide ever divulge anything of what an individual retreatant has shared with them. It is a safeguard to give the guide a space, too, to explore where God is for them in the experience of accompanying others.

It cannot be stressed too often, that the strictest confidentiality is maintained in every reputable retreat house, and anything you share with your guide remains only between the two of you.

Once the initial meeting is over, the silence usually begins, perhaps at about 8 or 9 o'clock on the first evening. From that point on, for the following six or eight days, you are asked to respect the silence within the house and its gardens. This is not an imposition or even a 'discipline' but a *gift* that retreatants offer each other. Often a silent retreat brings people into contact with the deeper reaches of themselves and their life issues. If another person interrupts this encounter, or begins to 'export' their own agenda, the process is disturbed.

Now that you are alone in the silence, the days are yours to shape as you will. The routine of mealtimes, worship and the daily meeting with your guide help to structure the day, but you may still be surprised to find how hard it can be, initially, to plan to use your time well. Your guide will be glad to help with this, if you ask, and will give you guidelines on finding a balance between rest, prayer and recreation, such as walking. Try to make space for all of these things. A time of retreat is a time to rest, and if you feel tired don't be afraid to lie down and sleep! God can speak to your heart just as effectively (perhaps more so) when you are asleep as when you are awake. Times of prayer can be planned too, if you wish. Your guide may suggest ways of incorporating periods of prayer into your day, helping you to decide how often, and for how long, you feel drawn to pray. Closeness to God is not, of course, limited to periods of deliberate prayer, and you will probably sense a deepening into God in everything you do. Enjoy the peace and the space. Really savour the food, and take advantage of the surrounding countryside. Use your senses to help you grow in awareness of everything around you. In a retreat you really do have the time to 'stand and stare', and to touch, taste and feel. Make the most of it. You will be amazed at what you notice, and in everything God is waiting to greet you in some way.

You may be feeling apprehensive about the time with your guide. Some of the commonly asked questions are addressed in Part II. Enough to say here simply that your guide is there just to be alongside you, as a listening friend, who is completely *with* you. The only Guide is the Holy Spirit. Your retreat companion is a privileged bystander, who will try to help you discern God's action in your prayer and your life just by reflecting back to you those things that seem to be touching you deeply. The daily meeting will normally not be for longer than half an hour. It is open space, in which you can share as much or as little as you wish. It may help you to get the most out of this meeting if you make a few notes as you go through the day about anything you feel you want to bring up at the meeting. It is the responsibility of the guide to keep an eye on the time, but please bear in mind that he or she will probably be accompanying several other people each day, so it is not a good idea to bring up the most important issue in the last two minutes of your meeting.

At the end of your meeting, the guide will normally suggest a focus for the next day's prayer, based on what you have shared. This will often be a passage of scripture, but may also be other material, such as a poem or a picture, or some form of prayer exercise, whatever your guide feels might be helpful to you personally. This does *not* mean that you are obliged to use this focus. Every retreat guide would assure you that you should follow the prompting of the Holy Spirit in your own heart, rather than adhering blindly to their suggestions. Any suggestions the guide offers are merely to help you move forward.

Mealtimes in silence are not as problematic as you might fear. Very often gentle background music will be played at the main meals, and the silence at table is friendly, co-operative and companionable. You will be surprised at how much can be communicated without words, and you may begin to be more lovingly observant of others, and they of you, than you would have believed possible. This nurturing silence prevails throughout the house, and is communicated by smiles and gestures that help people to become more – not less – aware of each other's needs.

Over the days of your retreat, you will probably find that you discover your own rhythm of rest, exercise and prayer, and you will begin to see something of the way God's encounter with you in this special time is evolving. Let God be God, in whatever is happening in your prayer and reflection. Some retreats are remembered in years to come as mountain-top experiences ripe with new insights and directions. Others are recalled as gentle times of quiet, simply being in the silence with God. Others, again, can be times of challenge and even of painful new growth. Trust God, in all that is happening, and entrust yourself to God's leading.

The silence of the retreat ends with breakfast on the final morning, following a full six, or eight days. You may find the chatter at breakfast quite disturbing after the days of silence, or you may welcome it as a needful halfway house between the retreat situation and your home routine. It may be hard to leave, or you may be glad to return to the world beyond the retreat house doors. Whatever your feelings, only the weeks and months and years ahead will reveal the fruits of what has been sown in your heart during these days of intensive prayer.

Take care as you journey home, especially if you are driving. The sudden transition from complete peace to the stress of city traffic can be a little traumatic. Drive slowly at first and give yourself plenty of space. Your reactions may not be as sharp as normal in this changed situation. And when you arrive home, you may find it helpful to adjust gradually, perhaps by giving yourself some space and silence, if possible during the course of the days ahead. The eruption of radio and television into your life again can jar, so take things gently.

Choosing a retreat centre

A glance through the pages of *Retreats* shows something of the scale of the choice, and, of course, not all retreat centres are listed there. So if you are thinking of making a residential retreat, how do you decide where to go?

Some considerations are offered below:

FULL-BOARD OR SELF-CATERING?

Your budget may well decide this question for you. Self-catering retreats are generally cheaper than full-board accommodation, for obvious reasons. Both have their advantages. In a self-catering retreat you have greater control over your own time, and you will not be disturbed by other retreatants even at mealtimes. On the other hand, providing yourself with meals is a task that you might like to be free of for a while. Self-catering retreats are often in small cottages or annexes to larger retreat houses. The sense of isolation is often stronger in this situation, which may be exactly what you want, or it may become oppressive. This depends a great deal on your own personality, and how comfortable you are in your own company.

SIMPLICITY OR LUXURY?

Again, this will often be a matter of cost. Most retreat houses aim to offer good, wholesome food, ranging from 'simple' to 'very satisfying'. A retreat house is not a luxury liner, and most people would not wish it to be so. In most centres there are tea and coffee making facilities available throughout the day and night, often in little kitchenettes close to the retreatants' bedrooms. Some of the larger houses are upgrading their accommodation to en suite. You may feel that the comfort and privacy that this affords is what you are looking for and are prepared to pay for. Or you may prefer more basic accommodation.

Often the *atmosphere* of a retreat house is more important to retreatants than the size or quality of their bedrooms. If the place exudes a feeling of welcoming warmth, and has a certain character that differentiates it from a boarding school, they will feel at home there.

The gardens and surrounding landscape can be an important factor in choosing a retreat centre. Most houses have gardens that are conducive to quiet reflection, and some are set in a beautiful landscape, among hills perhaps, or by the seashore. Look out for this if it is important to you to be able to go for walks straight from the retreat house door (without negotiating roads or having to drive). And if you do choose a retreat house with walking possibilities, don't forget your strong boots.

Guided or alone?

This section has described the typical course of a guided retreat. It is, of course, possible to make a retreat without having a guide alongside you, and some people prefer this. If this is your first retreat, however, you might be well advised to go for a guided retreat. The guide will not force him or herself on you if you would prefer not to take advantage of the daily meetings, but if you are completely alone, there is no choice. A guide can be a great source of strength if complicated issues come up for you, or if you hit a patch of desolation. It feels like having a friend around who is there for you if you need them or want to share with them, but will not intrude into your space.

However, the time may come when you feel that what you most need is a period of silence entirely on your own, in which case look for a retreat house that supports this requirement. The description in *Retreats* will indicate where this kind of retreat can be made.

Silent or not-so-silent?

Most individually given residential retreats are advertised as being conducted in silence. However, there are degrees of silence! There are some retreat houses that safeguard the silence better than others. This is not the kind of information you will discover in the books or leaflets. If it is important to you that the silence is truly respected throughout your retreat, you might do well to ask someone who has experience of different retreat houses to advise you.

The reaction to silence varies widely. Some people find it oppressive, and next time round will look for a more gregarious experience.

For others the silence becomes a haven that they seek out year after year.

As a general principle, you will find that the silence is more absolute in retreat houses that are devoted solely to the giving of silent retreats. If there are other events, such as courses, going on at the same time, the silence will inevitably be compromised a little, though people who are not in retreat will normally be asked to respect the quiet of those who are. In the best retreat houses you can depend on an atmosphere of silence even when retreats and courses are running concurrently, to the extent that meals will be offered at different times to those in retreat.

Looking for like-minded companionship?

For many people a retreat means a time for being together with others, in a prayerful environment, with the focus on some aspect of their journey with, and growth in, God. It is this focus, perhaps, that makes the distinction between a 'spiritual holiday' and a genuine retreat. In a holiday the focus is, quite legitimately, on the holiday-maker. In a retreat, the focus is on God, as retreatants seek to discern more deeply where God is active in their lives.

Intensive silence and solitary reflection is not everyone's way of doing this kind of discernment. And so a whole range of retreat opportunities has evolved, inviting pilgrims to be in 'a place apart' but to spend their time of retreat more actively, and with the chance to share this time with others. Retreats of this nature are often called **theme retreats**, and they come in a range of different shapes and sizes. Some of the most common types of theme retreat include:

- Retreats offering some instruction or guided reflection on a particular topic.
- Retreats offering space for people with particular needs, circumstances or difficulties to come together and share their experience, usually with a trained facilitator.

- Retreats providing prayerful space and time for the participants to pursue a chosen activity.

Typical examples include:

- Retreats focusing on justice and peace issues, on Celtic spirituality, Orthodox spirituality, Advent, Harvest or Lenten themes, or any aspect of the spiritual journey. These are also known sometimes as 'preached retreats', because they include definite periods of input or teaching from the retreat leader(s). Don't let this term put you off, however. If the retreat is properly and sensitively conducted, you should have no sense of being 'preached at', but you will be offered a particular line of thought or reflection (once or twice a day for up to an hour) with the aim of stimulating your own reflective process.
- Retreats for young people, people facing mid-life decisions, the retired, the divorced or separated.
- Retreats centred on activities such as calligraphy, embroidery, circle dancing, yoga, aromatherapy, the healing arts, painting, storytelling, music, drama, poetry or creative writing or journalling, or retreats aiming to impart a particular skill, such as the **Enneagram** or the **Myers Briggs Type Indicator**® **(MBTI**™**)**. 'Walking retreats' are also becoming increasingly popular, encouraging participants to enjoy the countryside (or indeed the cityscape) creatively and prayerfully.

What happens during a 'theme retreat'?

Theme retreats vary enormously in the way they are structured. Basically, however, a typical day will include time to engage in the topic or activity being explored, time for yourself, for quiet reflection, for recreation, or for simply resting and enjoying the peace, and time to be together, socially, with the other participants. In some cases there will be opportunities to speak privately with the retreat leader(s), but if this is important to you it is worth checking in advance that it will be possible.

Usually 'activity retreats' do not assume any previous knowledge or ability, and all are welcome. Many people who would say, for example, that they 'cannot draw' or 'write', or whatever, nevertheless greatly enjoy the opportunity to exercise their creativity without any demand to 'achieve' anything, but simply as a means of exploring what is going on in their own hidden depths. The opportunity to share something of this exploration with others who are on the same wavelength is one of the great benefits of this type of retreat and can be a powerful catalyst for personal growth. And sometimes lifelong friendships are formed during these periods.

Retreats for self-contained groups of people

It often happens that a number of people who already know each other well – perhaps from the same church or neighbourhood, or from an existing prayer group or group of colleagues engaged in the same kind of work – choose to make a retreat together, as a discrete group.

By its nature, such a retreat will normally be a theme retreat, focusing on some aspect of the common life and quest of the people in the group. The group will plan for the retreat, taking into account the various hopes and expectations of all concerned, just as a family might plan for a holiday together. Indeed, some retreats like this are called 'church holidays', but they have a strong spiritual focus and can therefore truly be regarded as retreats.

Let us look first at what we might call a church 'away weekend'. The people in the parish have decided, well in advance, where they would like to go and what they would like to do when they get there. They may have invited someone from outside the group to lead them in their reflections and prayer during the weekend. They will also have thought about the ages and the needs of the people who are coming. They will then have booked the venue – perhaps a country house somewhere, or a seaside hotel, or a more formal retreat centre.

A period of time away together like this can be enormously strengthening and enriching to the people who make it. A bonding can happen on retreat that goes beyond the normal interactions of group or parish life. Living together in community, and exploring together some aspect of their journey of faith, creates an opportunity for a new surge of growth, and can be a catalyst for new beginnings in the wider community from which the group is drawn.

The form of a group retreat like this will normally follow the same broad pattern as that described for theme retreats in general. There will be time for shared worship and prayer, for some kind of teaching or focus sessions, maybe led by an outside facilitator, and for shared leisure and maybe some social time.

If you are planning a group retreat of this nature, you might like to give some thought to the following considerations:

- *How many people are interested in making the retreat?* You will need to have some fairly definite idea of numbers before booking the venue, and this will imply a need for a degree of commitment by the participants. It will enable you to decide the cost per head, the necessary deposit, and the extent of the accommodation required.
- *Who is the retreat for?* Is it intended to offer a retreat, for example, to a group of people who have the same general expectations (such as a prayer group), or is this to be open to the members of a wider group (such as a parish community)? In the latter case, how are you going to provide for the needs of all age groups? If the retreat is to be accessible to young families, for example, there will need to be reliable child care available, and good leadership for children's and young peoples' activities, as well as the material for the 'adult sessions'. Bear in mind, if at all possible, that parents will appreciate some time to make something of a retreat themselves, free of the responsibility for their children, if only for an hour at a time, so plan to have some activities for the younger members of the group that are led by someone other than their parents. If a crèche is to be provided for babies and toddlers, this too needs careful pre-arranging. 'Bought in' help in this field can prove to be very expensive, but parents of the very small may be willing to arrange a rota for crèche duty.
- *What kind of focus is required?* Take care to choose a theme for the reflection sessions that will speak to all present. For a prayer group, or a group of colleagues working in the same environment, this will be relatively easy. For a parish group, ranging in age from newborn to centenarians, and across all ability ranges, it will be a much more challenging task to find the right focus,

and to find a speaker who will be sensitive to the diversity of the group. But the results can be well worth the effort.

- *What kind of balance is needed* between shared worship, study or reflection sessions and leisure time? Consult well in advance with those hoping to make the retreat, to establish a consensus on this, and draw up a plan well ahead of time. If the group includes all ages, a common pattern will be to leave every afternoon free for people to enjoy as they wish, and it may be helpful to arrange some impromptu entertainment at least on one of the evenings. This may be as simple as showing a video, or it may be the parish opportunity to put on its own show. There is a special quality of 'togetherness' when an evening can truly be enjoyed by everyone across the age range.

- *Cost management:* Aim to keep the costs within the range of the least privileged members of the community. Many retreat houses and Christian hotels are happy to welcome groups who are working to a strict budget, and will do all they can to keep costs to a minimum. Expenditure can also be eased by asking participants to share cars for the journey to and from the venue, and by planning to make the retreat in off-peak times of the year.

- *Consider making an audio recording of the main events and session of the retreat,* including the shared worship, for the benefit of those who were unable to join the retreat, and as an aid to ongoing reflections for those who were there.

Without a doubt, arranging a group retreat is hard work, especially if the retreatants come in all ages, but the fruits will not disappoint you. Again and again people return to their groups or parishes from group retreats with new energy and sharpened vision and enthusiasm that spreads out in ripples beyond the boundaries of the group itself. The seed that is sown in these retreats becomes seedcorn for fresh growth in the wider community.

Struggling with a problem?

Most of us find ourselves, at some stage in our lives, grappling with some difficulty that begins to wear us down, and can leave us feeling helpless and in need of a 'solution'.

'Solutions', however, are not what a retreat is about. A retreat is, first and foremost, about space, and about time. Space and time that may well enable us to reflect on the implications of a problem in our lives, and maybe, if we wish it, the opportunity to share something of our feelings and struggle with a listener, who will offer us non-judgemental empathy. What a retreat will *not* do is provide us with a 'fix'. Nor will a retreat companion attempt to solve problems or offer therapy.

A **retreat guide/retreat director** will have been trained, quite explicitly, not to try to solve problems. There are several excellent reasons for this.

First, retreat guides are simply companions. They are not normally trained to carry out psychotherapy, and they are not there as counsellors. They are there to walk alongside you, as a peer, during a part of your spiritual journey, and they will not step outside this range of competence, though, if appropriate they may sensitively suggest that you might benefit from specialized help, such as relationship or bereavement counselling.

Second, the only authentic solutions to personal problems are those we discover for ourselves. It may well be that in the course of your retreat some new direction suggests itself to you, or your perspective on a problem changes, bringing new light. The retreat guide will simply listen to anything you wish to share and reflect back to you the way your own mind and heart seem to be moving. Often, when we speak about a problem with someone else, we hear ourselves in a new way, and the problem is understood more clearly.

Nevertheless, you will certainly find retreats advertised for people with a particular difficulty, or those in a potentially painful situation in life. Examples include retreats specifically focused for the bereaved, the divorced, for gay people, or for those who are HIV-positive. The reason for this kind of focus is not to make the pain of difficult circumstances go away, but to offer a safe space where those in similar situations can come together, either in silence, or to share their journeying with each other.

Sometimes quiet days or weekends are offered for people affected by some kind of addictive problem, such as alcoholism or eating disorders. These may well provide workshops which give you space to explore your difficulty in a relaxed and accepting environment, but again, they will not offer any ready-made solutions. If they are well, and responsibly, organized and run they will usually make it clear, in their publicity, that they are not offering therapy.

To find out about the possibility of retreat days with this kind of focus, you might find it helpful, in the first instance, to contact one of the relevant support groups (such as Alcoholics Anonymous, or Anorexia and Bulimia Care) for any information about suitable days or weekends.

Looking for place and atmosphere?

For some people there is a powerful attraction of 'sacred place'. Something draws us to places that have been centres of prayer and meditation through the years, or even through the centuries. Such places seem to be 'soaked in prayer', and it can be especially helpful to be in such a place for a period of retreat.

Often this kind of retreat is the culmination of a pilgrimage. The journey to the sacred place is part of the retreat, and itself an act of prayer, often in the companionship of other Christians.

What happens, when you arrive at the destination of your pilgrimage depends, of course, on where you have journeyed to. You may choose to join in the life and worship of the community there (perhaps a monastery or an abbey, where you are welcome to share in the celebration of the daily office and maybe also in the household duties). Or you may prefer to spend the time simply being present to the natural world, for example of a holy island like Iona off the west coast of Scotland, or Lindisfarne off the north-east coast of England. Often there will be guide books and reflective notes to help you engage prayerfully with the place and its history.

Perhaps you only have a day to spare and are unable to travel far. Usually, if you look around you, and perhaps ask for guidance from your local library, you will discover that there is a 'sacred place' near to where you live. This might be a little-known hermitage, such as a cave that was once the dwelling of a holy person of prayer in centuries past, or perhaps a well that has been sought out by pilgrims through the ages. Or it might be a nearby medieval town, where it is possible to walk quietly around the landmarks, old and new, taking time to reflect on what they mean for you today. In Shrewsbury, for example, an excellent leaflet is available from the library and tourist centres, offering you spiritual food for a short prayerful walk around the town. And if no such guide is available, why not produce one for yourself, and for others who may be glad to follow after? Another example of sacred place is where deep feeling has been experienced, possibly following some great tragedy, or in an act of thanksgiving. The village of Eyam, in Derbyshire, has an atmosphere or sanctity, from its history of hero-ism at the time of the Great Plague, while in Coventry Cathedral the pilgrim can connect both to the anguish of loss and destruction and the joy of new life, springing from the ashes of war.

While not, strictly, a 'retreat', for many people a few days spent in a gathering place like the community of Taizé in central France is an experience of 'total immersion' in a sacred place. The opportunity to join in worship and workshops and quiet conversations with en-thusiastic believers from all parts of the world is a deeply inspiring way of moving forward along their own spiritual path with renewed joy and commitment.

If your search for sacred place and atmosphere is leading you abroad, you will, of course, find many possible destinations in Europe and worldwide. An organization called 'Retreats Beyond Dover' specializes in arranging retreats that combine a holiday abroad with time for reflection in sacred space. You will find details of opportunities like this in the *Retreats* magazine. For details of re-treats at local places of 'spiritual presence', approach the centre di-rectly or talk to someone who has been there, for a first-hand account.

Pilgrimage

Pilgrimage is a form of retreat that places the emphasis on journeying to a holy place. Some walking is usually involved, giving the retreat an element of asceticism, and providing opportunities along the way for prayer and reflection – either individually, or as a group, if several people are journeying together.

Typically, in Britain today, such pilgrimages head for sacred sites, often those made sacred by the presence of Celtic saints. The North-ern Cross is an example of a student pilgrimage to the island of Lin-disfarne. Students take it in turns to carry a large cross, in groups of four or five, and at the end of the pilgrimage, Easter is celebrated on the island.

To visit such sites is, for many, a life-giving experience, touching on deep levels of faith and prayer.

Walking retreats

Not everyone can take several days out to make a full-blown pilgrimage. For those who feel drawn to seek out a retreat space on their feet, but may only have a day to spare, a walking retreat may provide just what is needed. Walking retreats come in all varieties. Typically, the leader will introduce a theme, as a focus for the walkers' thoughts, and will then lead the walk – ideally ensuring that there is space, as it were, between the participants, to allow for uninterrupted private reflection at various stages along the route.

A very popular, and gentle, form of walking retreat might be summed up as a 'praying the season' day, during which the leader will take participants on a guided meditative walk, perhaps through the countryside, and encourage them to engage in a prayerful way with the season of the year and all that it might mean to them in their personal living.

Facing a major life choice?

Perhaps, like me, you can look back over major life decisions you have made in the past and wonder: 'What was I actually thinking of when I chose that course?' With hindsight, how often we wish that we had 'known then what we know now'. It might have saved us a great deal of heartache and disappointment.

Well, what we do know now is that big decisions are better made with God. So perhaps one way to approach a major life choice in the future might be to reflect deeply on the implications of the choice, in a time of retreat. Of course, a retreat will not grant us some inner vision of how our choices are going to work out in practice. But it will give us time to do some serious discernment about what we most deeply want, and which direction our inner wisdom will seek out, given the time and space to do so.

This kind of discernment lies at the heart of what is sometimes called 'The Long Retreat', or the 30-day (or even 40-day) retreat. If you are facing a big question in your life, perhaps about your future course of work, or commitment to a cause, or the decision to marry, or to have a family, or, less happily, to end a destructive relationship or leave an exploitative work situation, a sustained time of retreat may be what would help you most.

One of the most popular, and helpful, ways of making a long retreat involving discernment of a life choice is to use the model of the **Spiritual Exercises of St Ignatius Loyola**. These Exercises are structured in a way that encourages the retreatant to reflect on the implications of the choice in question, to make a decision, and to seek to confirm it through prayer. The journey of this retreat will usually be accompanied by an experienced **retreat guide/retreat director** who is familiar with the dynamic of the Exercises and will be able to listen, with you, to the promptings and movements arising in your heart from the days and weeks of prayer.

If a structured set of Exercises is not for you, however, there are other ways of taking significant time out in seclusion and silence, with or without a personal guide, and you will find some of the alternatives listed in the *Retreats* magazine.

A long retreat will follow a similar pattern as that of any form of **individually given retreat**. It will, however, normally be preceded by a few days of acclimatization, before the silence begins, to give you an opportunity to reflect on your journey so far, and what you are hoping for from the retreat, and perhaps to meet any other people who will be with you in retreat. And there will frequently be a few days after the retreat is over and the silence ends, to review the experience for yourself, and with others if you so wish. These final few days are also an important buffer zone between the silence of seclusion and the hustle and bustle of the daily life to which you will be returning. They help to reduce the shock of 're-entry'.

During the retreat itself, there will normally be three or four rest days, when the silence may be lifted, and you will be free to relax in your own way. For some people these days can feel like an intrusion into the silence; for others they are an essential loosening of the intensity of the experience. If you don't want to break your silence there is, of course, no compulsion to do so.

The days of the retreat progress as they would in a shorter, six- or eight-day individually given retreat. You will probably meet your guide once a day, and share with him or her anything that has come up in your prayer. The guide will offer you the next day's prayer material, based on what you have shared. If you are making the full Exercises of St Ignatius, you will probably be planning to make four or five periods of prayer each day, each period being around an hour, though your retreat companion will help you to discover what pattern of prayer suits you best. It must be said, however, that whatever pattern you choose, a retreat of this kind is an intensive undertaking, not to be entered into lightly.

Not everyone who has a major life choice ahead of them has the time or the money to disappear to a retreat house for 40 days. St Ignatius was well aware of this problem himself, and made sure that he and his companions also offered the **Spiritual Exercises in daily life**. The pattern of the prayer is the same as in a 30-day retreat, but instead of four or five hours' prayer each day for 30 days, the retreatant will normally be asked to make about an hour a day over to prayer and reflection, and will meet the guide once every week or every two weeks over a period of up to nine months. This experience, too, is a marathon, but the fruits far outstrip even the very significant effort put into it. It may be, of course, that the nature of any choices that are ahead of you only becomes clear as you move through the retreat. It is perfectly reasonable to make a long retreat without having a particular choice to make in it. Often people sense that they are at a crucial time of life, and feel the promptings of something undefinable, urging them to look at where they are and where they are going.

I am reminded of the moment in *The Wind in the Willows*, when Mole senses that his underground home is nearby and it is time to return to it for hibernation. He doesn't know, with his mind, what it is that is ruffling his consciousness, but he knows he has to follow these unconscious nudges. In the same way we can sometimes feel the nudgings of our hearts that may well be trying to tell us that it is time to step aside and ponder awhile.

It may be that the decision you are trying to make involves a vocation to the religious life or the priesthood. If so, there are a number of opportunities to test out your intuition by spending time in a religious establishment in the tradition you feel drawn towards. This experience, which may be as short as a weekend, or as long as several months, enables you to live with a community and explore your reactions with a guide.

Similarly, if you are contemplating marriage, there are opportunities to make 'marriage preparation retreats', or to make an individually given retreat along with your intended partner, with the option to see your guide either individually or together, or a mixture of the two or, indeed, to have separate guides during your retreat. The retreat itself will be focused on the impending decision or commitment, and your guide will suggest material for prayer that will help to dispose your mind and heart towards the necessary discernment.

Whatever the choice that lies ahead, the most helpful type of retreat to make in preparation is one in which you can reflect in silence, and explore your prayer individually with someone who understands where you are, and is familiar with the tools of spiritual discernment. And if you are intending to go away to a retreat house for this length of time, make sure that it is a place where you will feel at ease. It may help to visit it beforehand and talk to some of the staff, before you finally commit yourself.

PART II

The Questions You Didn't Like to Ask

The questions included in this section are among those actually asked by people thinking of making a retreat, perhaps for the first time. They are grouped under the following main headings: Ethical questions; Will I feel at home?; Relationship with the retreat guide; and Practicalities. The reflections offered here in response to these questions are based on my own experience both of making retreats myself and of accompanying others on retreat. They are personal responses, and should not be taken as definitive statements about topics that are by their nature deeply subjective.

Terms that are covered as topics in the Fact File in Part IV are indicated by the use of bold type.

Ethical questions

Isn't a retreat rather an individualistic, self-centred luxury?

This argument is commonly used by detractors to call into question the value, and even the ethical basis, for a retreat. A retreat, they claim, is an excuse to indulge in introspection, and it is an escapist activity, avoiding the realities of a world in trouble.

These complaints demand respectful attention. If they are true, they must be taken seriously.

For many people the entire 'spiritual journey', including all personal prayer, is open to the charge of 'unhealthy introspection'. So we must ask ourselves, what are we actually doing, when we attempt to move inwards to the 'core', or the 'ground of our being'? Is this drawing us further away from each other, in an attempt to come closer to God? Is it just a personalized spirituality, and if so, can this have anything to do with the kingdom of God?

I have grappled with this question myself, and I remain convinced that when we seek to go deep into the heart of ourselves, we also come closer to the heart of each other. In prayer, and especially in the intensive prayer of a retreat, we go down, as it were, to the bedrock of our own being. To sink into the core of our own being is also to deepen into that bedrock where we are mysteriously in touch with the core of all being the place where all is 'One'. The evidence for the truth of this lies in the effects it has: if we return to the everyday world after prayer more in harmony with creation and with all other beings, then the encounter at the bedrock has been creative in ways that will radiate outwards and be life-giving for others as well as for ourselves.

If this is so, then to make a retreat is not to escape from the 'real world', but to open ourselves up to our interrelatedness, and to see afresh anything that is blocking this wholeness. If we can really start to do this, we might begin to realize that things are the other way round: we are often 'escaping' from reality when we are so busy doing all the things we find so important in daily life, and we are facing and encountering a deeper Reality when we take time to stand still and to listen to the movements of our hearts.

If prayer and meditation, and sustained times of retreat, enable us to move closer to the core of our own being and to the core of all being, this movement has a purpose: we are empowered, in the depths of this 'core', to move *out* again with renewed energy and vision, and to turn our contemplation into action within a wounded world, and into choices and decisions that will contribute to our world's healing and whole-making.

As Christians we know that Jesus himself would frequently withdraw to a quiet place to pray, and his model is surely an invitation to us to do the same, in whatever ways we can. We also know that the need to withdraw into seclusion from time to time has always been a valued part of the Christian tradition. This seems to have been especially important at times of great trial or times when the light of the gospel values seemed to be dimming. Yet Jesus himself tells us: 'By their fruits you shall know them', and I believe we can, and must, apply this test to our 'retreating'. If it bears good fruit, for ourselves, for those around us, and for all creation, then it is of God. If it isolates us from others and from the needs of the world, then it is not of God. Each of us must discern this for ourselves.

Will I be 'brainwashed', or 'converted', or otherwise psychologically manipulated?

This is a common misconception about what happens during a retreat, and it is also a classic objection put up by hostile families trying to put people off the idea of leaving them alone for a week.

It would be easy to say that it *is* a misconception, and leave it at that, but it remains a genuine, and partly justified fear in people's minds, especially if they have never made a retreat before.

Tragically it is true that there will always be a small minority of people who seek to manipulate the hearts and minds, and ultimately the lives, of others, and religious institutions have historically been among the worst offenders in this respect.

As a general statement, it is true to assert that no bona fide retreat house exists to exert any kind of pressure on its guests. The purpose of all of them is to provide space where the individual can be helped to explore his or her relationship with God, in a setting that is quiet and conducive to prayer and reflection.

If you choose your retreat house carefully and prayerfully, perhaps asking for guidance from people who have some experience of making a retreat, you will not suddenly find yourself in the clutches of a coercive organization, bent on getting you to think and act as they do. This attitude would run counter to the whole idea of making a retreat, and it would be anathema to every sincere retreat guide.

In the extremely unlikely situation that you *do* find yourself in a place that seems to have a 'hidden agenda', you are free to leave it at any time, without giving any reason for your departure. If this should ever happen, and the retreat house in question was listed in the *Retreats* magazine, then the Retreat Association would want to hear from you about this kind of negative experience. While this association cannot take responsibility for every retreat house listed, it will not knowingly endorse any house that is seeking to exert influence of this kind on its guests.

The other possibility, however, is that, having booked into a retreat house, for an **individually given retreat**, you find that your own **retreat guide** seems to be trying to influence you in some way, to persuade you to follow a particular line of thought or make a decision in a particular way. Again, *this should never happen*. Retreat guides are trained not to get between God and the retreatant, and certainly never to seek to impose their own pet theories or allegiances. If you really feel that a retreat guide is trying to exert some kind of pressure on you, it is your right and your duty to protect yourself. It would be important to voice your misgivings, first to the retreat guide in person, if you can. If this is too delicate, you are free to approach the person who is co-ordinating the retreat. You are also free simply not to meet with your guide, and to let God guide your retreat without their help. You do not need to give any reason for your choice. If the guide has a problem with this, it is their problem and not yours!

These are, thankfully, very unlikely scenarios. When you enter into retreat, however, you are making yourself vulnerable, to an extent, before God and in what you share with your guide. God will never abuse this vulnerability, and neither will the vast majority of guides. Generally speaking, the interaction with a guide is self-regulating. Most people will only ever share what they feel safe in sharing, and most of us have a strong sense of whom we can trust and to what extent. We will open up our hearts where we sense the presence of God in the guide, and we will close down where we do not. This is the best protection against any kind of manipulation.

Remember too that the guide will be receiving regular **supervision**, and the supervisor will be watchful for any signs of a hidden agenda in the guide, and will help the guide to acknowledge this and deal with it, before it can affect anyone else.

What if my family is hostile to the idea?

It can happen that an individual feels strongly the need to make some kind of retreat, but other members of the family are less than enthusiastic. There are any number of reasons for this. Probably the most likely person to meet resistance to her hopes of making a retreat is the mother of the family. And much of the resistance may stem from the fact that while Mum is away, the rest of the family will have to fend for themselves. And indeed, it can be extremely difficult to get a family organized sufficiently to allow the 'breadbaker' to move out for a few days, but it may also prove to be a growth point for all concerned.

Again, if a working parent wants to make a retreat, this will usually mean that some part of the precious, and eagerly awaited 'annual leave' will be surrendered to what can look like a selfish desire on the part of one family member to do his or her 'own thing', at the expense of the family holiday. Balancing the relative priorities in this situation can be very difficult. If the situation is genuinely 'either/or' it may be necessary to postpone a separate residential retreat until the children are older. The time of childhood, and family holidays, slips by all too quickly, and 'babies don't keep'! On the other hand, if there are difficulties that a time in retreat might help to illuminate, the sacrifice of a week's holiday might prove to be a sound investment for the whole family.

Sometimes the resistance goes even deeper than this. Perhaps one partner needs to make a retreat because his or her spiritual journey is deepening and growing, and this in itself can appear very threatening to the other partner. We all evolve at our own pace, and the problem of life partners who find themselves 'out of sync' with each other's growth at various stages of their relationship is well known. This kind of mismatch requires very delicate handling if the legitimate needs of each partner are to be honoured. A few suggestions are offered below:

- If you are hitting serious resistance at home, and sense that this is about more than merely 'who will cook my supper when you're away?', consider making a **retreat in daily life** in the first instance. This will give you good space to reflect on your journey, to share it with a **prayer companion/prayer guide**, and to grow in your own personal inner freedom. It may also help the resisting partner to recognize that your spiritual journey is not as threatening to him/her as it first seemed. You may very well find that a daily life retreat will help to free you from your own fears, to discern where you need to confront any resistance and where it would be more fruitful to accept it and work with it, remembering that everything is always moving on, and this year's blocks may become next year's gateways.
- It might be possible to make a retreat away from home for just a short period at first – maybe a weekend or a few days only. It is much easier to organize a family to run on its own for two or three days than for six or eight days. And if you go away on retreat, and return to the family enriched and in deeper harmony with yourself (as you almost certainly will!) they will see for themselves that what they feared was not so fearful after all, and it may well be possible to make a longer retreat at a later stage.
- If the root of the resistance is in the partner's fear that you may be 'changed' or 'manipulated' while you are away, it might be worth considering suggesting that both you and your resistant partner make a short retreat together. Some retreat houses offer special weekends for couples (including 'same sex couples'), or 'taster retreats' over a weekend. Sharing the experience in this way, at least initially, can help to dispel any fears there may be.
- If your partner is resistant in general to any prolonged absence from home, or any separate activity, then there is a problem that goes beyond merely the question of making a retreat. Where one partner in a relationship is looking for space to explore his or her life questions independently, and the other is finding this deeply threatening, there may be a need for some form of relationship counselling. If you find yourself in this situation, and feel

that you really need the space that a residential retreat can give, it may take a lot of courage to make up your mind to go. However, though there are no guarantees, a genuinely spiritual retreat, with a sensitive **retreat guide**, may give you the very space you need to step back, to look at whatever problems there may be, and to move forward in a more enlightened way when you return home.

Will I feel at home?

I thought retreats were for priests and nuns. Wouldn't a lay person feel out of place?

It is very true that until about 30 or so years ago the possibility of making a retreat wasn't one that would cross many lay people's minds.

Those brought up in Roman Catholic schools will probably remember that an annual retreat was part of the curriculum for some, but the experience of these school retreats was not something shared by the large majority of people. Whatever retreats there were in those days were, on the whole, so-called 'preached retreats', which meant that people would assemble in groups – often quite large groups – to hear a speaker, usually a priest, discuss a particular subject, and then they would disperse to think over what they had heard.

Even among those in religious orders, 'preached retreats' of this nature were the norm. A time set aside for, as it were, special instruction, to focus their minds in particular ways.

Then a sea change occurred. Beginning in North America, but rapidly spreading to the United Kingdom, enthusiasm began to gather for what has become known as the **individually given retreat**. At first, this too was offered mainly by priests and mainly for the benefit of clergy and those in religious orders, but in a relatively short time the possibility of making such a retreat was opened up to all Christians, and indeed to those of other faiths or people with no religious allegiance.

This vision has led to the emergence of a large number of retreat houses, some with just a couple of rooms, some with over a hundred, where retreatants can spend time in stillness, with the availability of a trained companion if they wish.

Now, therefore, it is very common for those arriving at a retreat house to make a retreat to be lay people, and even people who are not attached to any institutional church. There is a 'radical equality' in a retreat. The bishop may be in the next room to the shop assistant and the coal miner, and the **retreat guide** may also be a lay person, from any walk of life, of either gender. In a **retreat in daily life** it is even more likely that the majority of retreatants, and most of the **prayer companions/prayer guides**, will be lay people.

If you make an individually given retreat, you will probably not know anything about the church background or status of your fellow retreatants, especially now when priests or those in religious orders will rarely be wearing distinctive dress, at least not during their time in retreat. These superficial distinctions truly become irrelevant where all are making a journey, each in his/her own way, to the core of their being.

I'm not a practising Christian. Does it matter?

This question is answered very simply, by a resounding 'No. Not at all!'

But a little more might also be mentioned on this question. It actually contains two components, which have the makings of two different questions:

- I'm not a Christian, or
- I'm not practising.

If you are not a Christian, have no allegiance to the Christian faith, and no sympathy with what we might call the Christic vision of life, then you might find a **theme retreat** that is focused on a particular aspect of Christian faith or practice would not speak to you. There are, however, many theme retreats that look at issues that go beyond the traditional boundaries of 'Christian faith', and you might well find one of these both interesting and challenging.

If you are not a Christian, but decide to make an **individually given retreat** in a Christian retreat house, you will probably have made your position known in advance, and your **retreat guide** will be more than happy to be alongside you wherever you are. All that is necessary, for your own sense of 'at-home-ness', is that you yourself should feel comfortable knowing that the house where you will be staying is a Christian one. There should be no attempt whatever to 'convert' you. The guide's task in an individually given retreat is merely to accompany the pilgrim, sharing the delights and the difficulties of the journey, whatever they happen to be. Guide and pilgrim meet as peers, fellow travellers on a spiritual journey. The absence of a commonly held 'creed' or doctrinal base should make no difference to this process, which is conducted in mutual respect. Many of the retreat guides I know personally would be delighted to have the privilege of walking alongside a pilgrim of another faith, or of none, during a retreat.

Whether, as a Christian, you are 'practising' or not, whether you go to church every day, or haven't been inside a church since the last family wedding, makes absolutely no difference to the welcome and the acceptance you can expect whatever type of retreat you choose.

Are retreat houses mainly for people of their own denomination? Will I feel out of place if I'm from a different denomination, or from none at all?

The simple answer is also an ambiguous one: Yes, it is probably true that most retreat houses are run by people belonging to one particular Christian denomination, but it is also true that the great majority of them are also actively ecumenical in their approach and attitude. This is because, in its deeper reaches, prayer is always ecumenical, in that it takes us to depths of our being that lie well below the fences that appear to divide us. And retreat houses are primarily about the prayer that unites us, not about the doctrines that divide us.

If you look through the pages of the *Retreats* magazine you will notice that most of the entries indicate which denomination runs the centre, but you will very often also see words like 'Welcomes those from all denominations or from none'. And in most residential retreats there will be a mix of Christians from all traditions. After a short time in retreat, among others who are seeking God as you are yourself, you will forget about the divisions of name or doctrine or practice that still come between us in the outside world, and feel increasingly at one with them in the deeper quest for God in our lives and our world.

In the United Kingdom, many of the retreat houses are either Roman Catholic or Anglican foundations, and they conduct their worship, for example, in line with these traditions. This means that in a Roman Catholic retreat house, the daily (or Sunday) Eucharist will take the form of a Catholic Mass. In an Anglican foundation an Anglican Eucharist will be celebrated, and so on. There are, how-ever, an increasing number of Free Church foundations offering re-treat space or opening up their premises for people to find quiet time, and the Quaker houses are, of course, well known as traditional oases of stillness. Whichever type of retreat house you choose, the team of retreat guides may very well be an ecumenical one, and the worship itself will be as inclusive as it is possible to be. Many more people from a Free Church background, for example, are now making retreats, and most feel in no way out of place in a Roman Catholic or Anglican retreat house.

Whether you choose to receive communion during a celebration of the Eucharist that is not in your own tradition, is up to you. Very few priests will refuse communion to anyone who comes for-ward in sincerity of heart, whatever their tradition. And all will agree that the prime authority in making such decisions is the Holy Spirit within us, and it is the promptings of this Spirit that we should follow.

Even in retreats, or weeks of seclusion, during which you are in-vited to share in the daily office of a particular religious order, you will find this same inclusive spirit. The worship will be offered within the tradition of the house, but all will be welcomed equally to participate in it.

Will I be expected to know the Bible?

Normally a **retreat guide** will expect nothing from the retreatant except an openness to make a journey of discovery and discernment of the ways in which God is acting in their lives.

Frequently an **individually given retreat** will make use of scripture. Your guide may suggest passages you might like to take as a focus for your prayer, but if so you will be given the references so that you can easily find the piece that is intended. In this kind of scripture-based prayer, what is important is to allow the words of scripture, or the events of the gospel and other scriptural stories, to touch *your own lived experience*. Scripture becomes a gateway to a personal encounter with God, and whether or not you are familiar with the structure and contents of the Bible is far less important than your openness to allowing scripture to reveal connections between your own life and the word of God.

In a **theme retreat**, too, the retreat guide will not normally be expecting any particular familiarity with the Bible. If he or she uses scripture during the retreat, perhaps in the course of the talks or as a focus for personal prayer in the quiet time, any necessary reference will be clearly given.

If you have a favourite version of the Bible, it may be helpful to take it with you on retreat. If biblical references are suggested, don't panic if you don't know where to start to look! Bibles always have a list of contents at the front, and most of us need to use it.

One of the most moving experiences I have ever made was while I was accompanying someone on an individually given retreat in daily life. At the end of our first meeting I suggested a couple of references that this person might like to look at and meditate with. The next week, the retreatant told me, very honestly, that he had not even known the difference between the Old and the New Testament, but that he had managed to find the psalms I had suggested, using the contents list. As the retreat progressed, I was to discover that this person was being drawn into very deep and life-changing prayer, and was powerfully affected by the connections he was finding in scripture with his own experience. Some of God's closest friends have never 'read the book'!

Why is silence expected and how will I cope with it?

Silence is only expected, or requested, during a silent retreat, usually an **individually given retreat**, or during parts of a **quiet day** reserved for silent prayer and reflection.

This kind of silence should not be regarded as an imposition or, worse, as some form of ascetical practice. Rather, it is a gift that we offer to each other, as people seeking a place to be still and to reflect on the presence and action of God in their lives. When we offer each other a time of silence, we are also offering the gift of space – 'sacred space' – where we undertake not to disturb each other's quiet by opening up conversations.

The silence respects and protects each person's space and privacy, and ensures that no one retreatant can undermine another's retreat by talking about his or her own agenda.

Silence can be disturbing in its own way, of course. Some people find a silent retreat a time of great challenge. Without the comforting distractions of normal background noise, or of radio and television, we come closer to recognizing our true selves, our real needs, our dependencies, and the demands of living for a while with just ourselves and God. But that is the whole point – to free ourselves of these many 'hooks' to which we may find we are more attached than we thought we were, and to be free to move forward to wherever the God within us is inviting us.

The silence in a retreat house has a special quality, however, and most people discover very quickly that it is not a threatening silence at all. On the contrary, it creates an ambience which in some ways bonds the retreatants, and their guides, closer together. When we cannot use words to greet each other, or to express our needs (at table for example), or to convey empathy, we are obliged to use a deeper kind of language. We become much more aware of people's gestures, their facial expressions, the language of their eyes, and so on, and much more sensitive to their needs.

Some people feel, at the end of a silent retreat, that they know their fellow retreatants more deeply than if they had been able to speak with them in the normal way. The gift of silence has led us not only to the core of our own being, but to the core of the being of those around us, in ways we cannot – but do not need to – express.

Different people deal with silence in different ways. If you are not used to any silence at all in your life, it might be wise to try a **first time retreat** for a weekend or just two or three days before you commit yourself to a week or more in silence. In a taster retreat like this you will have several hours of silence each day, but there will also be opportunities to talk, and to share experience with others. This will give you a sense of how you personally react to the effects of silence.

As a simple (though not exhaustive) test of how your particular personality might deal with being alone in silence for several days, you could try asking yourself these questions:

- When I am with a crowd of people, maybe at a party, or in some kind of group activity, do I tend to come more alive, the more I am with them, or do I find I need to withdraw at some stage, to get a bit of quiet, and re-collect myself? If the second pattern is more 'you', it might indicate that your natural way of gaining the energy you need for living is more likely to be found in a source of quiet solitude than from being among other people. It might suggest that you are a natural 'introvert', in which case you will probably deal well with silence, and benefit from it even though it may seem strange in the beginning.
- When I find myself alone for any length of time, do I tend to come more alive, or do I eventually feel a pressing need to be with others again, and rejoin the hustle and bustle of social life? If you identify more with this second pattern, it may indicate that your natural way of gaining energy is from being with other people, and from your interactions with them, and that extensive solitude eventually has the effect of diminishing your energies. This would be the pattern of a natural extrovert, who might find it harder to deal with the extended silence of a secluded retreat.

Both of these patterns are equally valid. God deals with his creatures as they are, extrovert or introvert. But it may be worth considering choosing the kind of retreat that more closely matches your natural patterns. If you feel that you veer more towards the 'extrovert' model, you might find a **theme retreat** a better first step. If you feel you veer more towards the 'introvert' model, a silent retreat may suit you very well.

Whatever personality type you feel you are, your **retreat guide** will help you make the most of your time in retreat, including using the times of quiet.

What happens if I 'fall apart' in solitude?

Solitude isn't something everyone feels at home with. This isn't a 'fault'. It is a matter of personality type. Generally speaking, an extrovert personality gains energy from being with people, and can find it draining when alone, especially in silence. An introvert personality is more likely to find solitude energizing, and feel drained of energy when compelled to be among large groups of people for any length of time. Having said that, many extroverts enjoy the solitude of retreat and find it refreshing and energizing, and some introverts find that they don't feel comfortable in the deep solitude of a silent retreat.

It can therefore happen that a person embarks upon a silent retreat, only to discover that the solitude feels oppressive. Very occasionally people experience real difficulty with the solitude.

One of the blessings, and the safeguards, of an **individually given retreat** is that you will always have a companion who is deeply committed to looking after you in every way while you are on retreat. This is part of what is expected of a **retreat guide**. It is, in part, a ministry of hospitality. So if it all gets too much, and you want to flee from the silence, talk it through first with your guide.

There are a number of reasons why this can happen. The most common is that the silence can reveal an emptiness, or an aching, or some kind of truth that we would rather not know about. You and your guide together may be able to look at this possibility and decide on the best course of action: whether to move very gently into the source of the problem, or whether to leave things alone.

It may be that there are other, more external, matters troubling you and disturbing the more fruitful potential of the solitude.

Difficulties that you have left at home, for example, such as some family problem or hostility, which is haunting your retreat. Again, do talk it through with your guide. Don't suffer in silence. Sometimes problems of this nature can be resolved by a well-timed phone call. Sometimes they need exactly the kind of distance that a retreat affords. Only you can know, but your guide can help with this kind of discernment, and offer you the moral support you need.

Or it may be that your personality simply reacts badly to solitude, in ways that you couldn't have predicted. If, having talked it through with your guide, you decide that you really don't want to make this silent retreat after all, remember always that you are a free being, and you can leave at any time. No one will put pressure on you to stay in a situation you don't feel comfortable in, and no one will think any the less of you if you make this decision.

And if the 'prayer time blues' come over you in a sudden wave of despondency, let your guide know at once. Most guides in a residential retreat will make themselves available at odd hours of the day or night if there is a genuine need. Normally a guide will be able to sense when this kind of desolation is brewing up in a retreatant, and will be vigilant for you, even if this is not apparent to you at the time.

But, as they say at the end of the crime prevention programmes on television: 'Don't have nightmares. This kind of problem is very rare indeed.' The vast majority of people find their time in solitude extremely fruitful, and they rapidly realize that the 'solitude' is actually being held in a warm and loving, though mainly wordless, companionship.

Do I have to be 'holy' all the time, or can I read a novel, listen to my Walkman, watch television, etc.?

So what does 'holy' mean? Something to do with 'wholeness', which in turn is pretty inclusive. Nevertheless, there is a sense of 'holiness' in most retreat houses that isn't so obvious in our daily lives. Some of this atmosphere of holiness is authentic. It is an atmosphere of prayer, and of people truly searching for, and experiencing, what lies deepest in their hearts. And not just the people who are living there this week, or this year, but often an atmosphere that has been generated over centuries of prayerful withdrawal and renewal. Then again, some of this 'holy atmosphere' can be less authentic, and seems to come from a sense of imposed or affected 'piety' that people put on like a cloak because they think that is how they are supposed to behave in a retreat house. There is nothing wrong with this, *unless* it becomes an aim in itself, and distracts us from the purpose of the retreat, which is always to grow more fully into our true selves before God.

Perhaps the first thing to reflect on is whether the everyday occupations we engage in are any less 'holy' than the attitudes we adopt when we are 'officially praying'. Reading a novel, listening to music, watching a good play, can all lead us closer to God as surely as an hour of adoration in the chapel. In principle, therefore, there is nothing wrong with any of these things (even during a retreat), provided they are not distracting you – or anyone else – from the underlying desire to engage with God more deeply in retreat than might be possible in everyday life.

And that is the heart of the matter: very often it is easier to pick up a book, or to tune in to the radio or television, than it is to be still, and allow yourself to sink deep into the core of your being, where you will be better able to discern the action and movements of God in your heart and in your life. If you are feeling the need, especially during an individually given retreat, to read, or to engage in other activities such as using a Walkman or watching television, it might be wise to talk through your feelings with your retreat guide, who will be able to help you discern whether these activities, in your particular case, are potentially helpful, or potentially distracting.

The empty space that results from not reading, not listening to the radio and not watching television may feel daunting, and the temptation to fill it up may be overwhelming at first, but remember that this is the space where God will reveal himself, and think twice before putting up the roadblocks. Try to keep yourself as open as possible to the power of prayer and of the uninterrupted stillness – not because others will expect it of you, but because it is in that *stillness*, and apparent emptiness, that you are most likely to discover what you have come on retreat to find.

Should I go on retreat alone, or with a friend?

If you are thinking of making a retreat for the first time, the thought of going alone can be daunting. If you have a friend who is also eager to make a retreat, then to go together seems like the obvious solution.

There are advantages and disadvantages, both in going alone and in going with a friend. Certainly a friend can provide moral support, and make it easier to go through all the apparent hurdles of settling into the routine of a retreat house for the first time. Especially for a **theme retreat**, the presence of a friend can be very beneficial, and a source of encouragement to both parties.

If you are intending to make an **individually given retreat**, the constant proximity of a personal friend can, however, become a distraction. It is hard to maintain silence around a close friend, for example, and it is very tempting to compare notes on how the retreat is going. This can all too easily develop into mutual sharing of experience during the days of the retreat itself, which can seriously deflect the course of the retreat journey of either or both of those concerned.

The situation can become even more complicated if partners make a retreat together. This happens not infrequently, and if this is genuinely what they both desire, there will be no objection from most retreat houses. However, discipline will be needed, to ensure that each person really does find the quietness and independence of movement that is needed if spiritual issues are to be fully explored. Sometimes partners or close friends come to a compromise solution, for example by agreeing to stay away from each other for part of the day, but to meet for a time, perhaps to go for a walk together.

Most retreat houses will arrange for partners or close friends who have come on retreat together, to have different **retreat guides**. This is because your retreat guide is there very much for *you*, and it is unhelpful if he or she is also unconditionally 'there' for someone else whose agenda may overlap (not always painlessly) with your own.

A special case arises, of course, when two people need to make a retreat together because one of them needs the continuing physical care and support of the other. Most retreat houses will be happy to advise and help you (for example, by offering shared or adjacent rooms), if you find yourself in this situation.

If you particularly wish to make a retreat with a partner, and the relationship between you is part of the agenda you are bringing to the retreat, you might like to consider making a retreat specifically designed for 'couples'. Some retreat houses do offer special weekends for married couples, and/or for those in same-sex relationships. The *Retreats* magazine listings will give you guidance on finding such retreats.

Relationship with the retreat guide

How can anyone else 'guide' me in prayer?

I often wonder, as I look around a group of people about to begin an **individually given retreat**, whether this is perhaps the one burning question they might like to ask, but usually don't. Certainly it is a question I frequently ask myself: 'What do we think we are doing when we offer ourselves as companions to other people along their spiritual journey?'

However, there was one memorable occasion when this question was indeed asked. A participant in a **retreat in daily life**, when asked 'Does anyone have any questions?' stood up and addressed the team of **prayer companions/prayer guides**: 'What makes you think you can teach us to pray?' Needless to say, we were floored by the question – me especially, since it was my first experience of prayer guiding following my training!

But the question did at least force us to focus on what we are really doing – and more importantly, what we are not doing, when we accompany another person in prayer.

It might be worth spending a few minutes just looking at some of the things that prayer guiding is *not* about:

- It is certainly not about teaching someone else to pray!
- It is not about trying to steer the other person's prayer in a particular direction.
- It is not about imposing any particular method of prayer, or approach to prayer on another person.

- It is not an excuse to preach at the pilgrim, to share the prayer companion's own agenda or to impart his or her own 'wisdom' (real or imagined!) to the pilgrim.

What it *is* about, however, is:

- Being alongside another pilgrim as they reflect on their personal prayer and their journey with God.
- Listening intently and lovingly, and with full attention, to all that the pilgrim freely chooses to share.
- Reflecting back any moments in the sharing where the pilgrim seemed to be especially stirred in some way.
- Providing free and non-judgemental space where the pilgrim can explore these moments more deeply if he or she so chooses.
- Offering guidance on various approaches to prayer if the pilgrim requests this or appears to welcome it.
- Offering suggestions as to how the pilgrim might like to focus their attention in prayer in the days that follow the meeting, but leaving the pilgrim completely free to follow up these suggestions or not.

The word 'guide' is in many ways a misnomer. The relationship between you and your prayer companion/prayer guide or **retreat guide** is more like that of two people taking a walk through the countryside. One of these people is the discoverer, sharing the experience in words and gestures with the other. The other is there simply to be alongside, noticing the reactions and responses of the first, and affirming all that seems to be leading to growth and insight.

So it might happen, during a country walk, that we stop to admire a particular view, or to notice some creature or some plant along the path, or just to take deep breaths of the fresh air. Or we may become aware of the weather, good or bad. We may move into conversation during this walk. Calmed by the serenity of the setting, we may open up issues that are active in our normal daily life, especially if we sense that we can really trust our companion.

And these are the kind of things that might happen in our 'walk' through the days or weeks of our retreat, in relationship with the guide. The guide is not there, in any sense, to 'show us the way', but to listen as we reflect on what is touching us especially in the current landscape of our lives. To be with us in those moments when something we discover really captures our imagination and reveals something of where God is for us. To help us to notice these things more intently for ourselves.

To play back what he or she is hearing in a way that helps us to hear it anew for ourselves. Someone once remarked: 'How can I know what I mean until I hear myself say it?' And this wisdom is one of the keys to so-called 'prayer guiding'. The guide is there to provide the space for you to hear yourself saying what matters to you, and to reflect back what has been heard in a way that helps you to come closer to where God is active in it all.

I don't find it easy to 'open up' to others. Will I have to do this?

The first thing to stress is that whatever kind of retreat you choose, it is *your* retreat, *your* special time with God, and it is *your* choice how you use this time. There should never be any question at all of your feeling pressured to talk about things you would rather keep to yourself, whether in a **retreat in daily life**, a **faith sharing meeting**, or an **individually given retreat** in a retreat house.

If you really do find it difficult in principle to talk openly with another person, and to build up this level of trust and confidence, it might be better, initially at least, to choose a **theme retreat**, rather than an individually given retreat. The former is an opportunity to deepen aspects of your Christian journey by listening to a speaker, following his or her suggestions by way of reflective exercises or approaches to prayer, and only sharing with others in the group, or with the retreat leader, if you specifically choose to do so. You will not normally experience any kind of pressure to share. If you do, you have every right to resist it!

In an individually given retreat, the focus is on your individual prayer, and the reflections on that prayer, which you are able to share with your guide to the extent to which you feel comfortable – and no further. It is the task of the **retreat guide** to build up an atmosphere of trust that encourages you to be as open as you can in what you share of your experience. The retreat guide is also trained to be very sensitive to the reactions of the retreatant, to read the unspoken signals and be responsive to them. The guide should be able to sense where you are open to sharing and where you would rather hold back. Every guide knows that there will be some retreatants who choose to share very little, while others will be almost unstoppable. People are very different, and you will not be expected to be any other than who you are!

Sometimes, when we are reflecting deeply on what matters most in our lives, we reach a point where we feel we really want to go on in our explorations, but don't quite know how, or don't quite yet have the courage to do so. If your guide detects such a moment, he or she may, very gently, encourage you to 'unpack' a little, but will do so by using open questions (questions that don't presuppose any specific kind of answer, or indeed, any answer at all), or by reflecting back something that you yourself may have said. It is then entirely your own choice, as to whether you follow up this invitation or not. The guide doesn't mind either way, and will not pursue anything that you don't pick up for yourself. Silence is a totally acceptable response at any stage, and so is a simple statement that you don't want to say any more about a particular matter. Remember that in every conversation with your guide, it is you who sets the agenda.

What will my retreat guide expect of me?

It is understandable, and perhaps inevitable, that when we go on retreat, even though we may have made retreats many times before, we feel a bit anxious about our encounter with the **retreat guide**. Who will it be? And will we hit it off together? Will I make a fool of myself? The questions go round and round in our heads.

We may need to turn this question round and ask ourselves: *What do I think* the guide will expect of me? And in reply to ourselves, we may discover that we are afraid, for example, that the retreat guide may be expecting us:

- To be at a so-called 'mature' stage of our spiritual journey
- To know what we want
- To be familiar with different forms of prayer
- To be in the habit of regular personal prayer
- To be very sure of our faith, and 'without doubts'
- To be able to articulate our deepest feelings
- And so on ...

Any or all of these things may come to haunt us as we approach a retreat. Let us first of all lay them all to rest, with the assurance that no retreatant (including retreat guides themselves when they make their own retreats) would ever get a very high score on expectations like these. And then let us look at these common misconceptions one by one:

- There is no such thing as a 'mature Christian'. We are all the merest beginners on the spiritual journey, and Jesus assures us that this is the best possible place to be 'as little children'.
- It is a rare individual who knows what he wants. And if she does, this may be because her mindset is closed to the possibility of growth and discovery. Not to know what you want is to be open to discovering layer upon layer of your desires, until you reach the depths where your own desires meet God's desire for you.
- There are as many forms of prayer as there are people seeking to pray. Your guide will accompany you wherever you are.
- Regular personal prayer is an ideal that many long for and few attain in practice. A retreat is a time to explore our *desire* for prayer, not to demonstrate our imagined achievements.
- Doubts are often the gateway to new growth, while fixed certainties can prevent that growth. It has been said that the opposite of faith is not doubt, but certainty.
- The deepest feelings usually defy words. Your guide will be alongside you when words fail, reading the signals of your heart. The stumbling searcher will often come closer to his own truth than the smooth verbalizer. God speaks through the gaps in our self-expression, and your guide will be tuned in to those gaps as much as she is tuned into the things you do say.

We have almost all grown up in a culture that measures our personal value to a certain extent by our 'achievements'. It would be naive to think that we can shed this mindset instantly when we are on retreat. But that, really, is what we have to do. As soon as you step over the threshold into your place of retreat you are stepping right back from the world that measures you by your qualifications and certificates. So the simple fact is that your retreat guide will not be expecting anything of you.

Every retreat guide will start from the premise that this is *your* time, *your* retreat – space in which to explore your personal relationship with God in whatever way you feel prompted to do. The guide will *hope* for an openness of heart, towards God, and towards whatever possibilities unfold during your prayer. But there will be no expectation at all of, for example, familiarity with scripture, with theology, with the practices of any particular tradition or with prayers of one type or another. The guide will not expect any predictable pattern of prayer, and will be completely open if, instead of praying with the material he or she has suggested, you have felt the urge to play the guitar all afternoon, or draw pictures, or play with clay. You are free to burst into song, or to burst into tears, to break out in joyful praise or to break out in an eruption of anger. All that the guide is trained to expect is the unexpected.

What will I talk about with my retreat guide?

Most people, at the beginning of their first retreat, are convinced that they will never find enough to say to the **retreat guide** to fill the 30 or 40 minutes scheduled for the one-to-one meetings. And after the first meeting or two, most are wondering how on earth they are going to fit it all into such a relatively short time.

But let us begin with those worries. For one thing, the one-to-one meeting *may* last as long as 30 minutes or more, but it *need* not. As the retreatant it is for you to decide how long you want to stay in conversation with your guide, up to the maximum that time permits. If you have shared all you wish to share in the first ten minutes, and your guide senses that you are ready to end the meeting, then that's fine.

Having said that, most people find that they have more to say

THE QUESTIONS YOU DIDN'T LIKE TO ASK

than they believed they would. For some this may be the first time that another person has really listened to then, and taken seriously their feelings about their spiritual journey. Such a listener encourages us to open up our deeper thoughts and feelings, hopes and fears, and once trust has been established between the guide and the retreatant, the conversations begin to take on a life of their own. The problem is more likely to be the need to focus on what you really want and need to say, and explore thoroughly what you most need to explore, than on filling the time.

So what is appropriate material for these conversations. Simply: 'anything and everything'! The conversations with your guide are primarily focused on whatever has arisen in your prayer and reflection during the previous day. But this prayer will be reflecting some aspect of your spiritual journey, which in turn is about the *whole* of you. There may be issues in your life or your relationships that come to mind in your prayer and that you would like to talk through with a sensitive listener. There may be doubts or hopes regarding your faith, or insights arising from what you have been praying about. And your guide will also be able gently to encourage you to explore any areas that appear to be important to you, and perhaps open doors for you to take the conversation further.

And what if, at the first meeting, you simply don't know where to begin? Well probably your guide will have suggested something on which to focus your first day's prayer, which may in itself spark off some line of exploration in your heart. Otherwise, it might be helpful to share with the guide something of how your faith journey has been so far, what have been the most obvious landmarks along the way, and where does it seem to be leading you right now. Your guide will help these early conversations to take shape, by encouraging you to feel at ease, and perhaps opening up a few general questions, in a non-threatening way.

What happens if I don't feel easy with my retreat guide?

The opening meeting of the retreat has taken place, and you have been given the name of your **retreat guide**. Whether in a **retreat in daily life**, or in a residential **individually given retreat**, you will probably not have had any choice about who your guide is to be. There is an understandable anxiety about how you will get on with this person who is to accompany you through your retreat, and with whom you will, potentially, be sharing something of the things that matter most to you in life.

One of the odd things about retreat-making and retreat-giving is that when two people are walking on the holy ground of the retreatant's personal experience in prayer and in life, the normal tendencies to like or dislike each other seem not to apply. People who might be perceived as irritants, if you met them at a party, give no such impression when they are sharing the deeper reaches of their hearts. It sounds like a cliché but it also happens to be true, that there is an almost instinctive positive regard for a person who is entrusting something of their deepest dreams to you. It can happen that, in general conversation, a particular person is being maligned, but if anyone is present who has ever accompanied that individual in prayer, that person will defend them to the limits. Perhaps something of God's unconditional love shapes the interaction between two people who are consciously seeking God's way together.

So it is actually not very likely that you will not get on with your retreat guide. Much less likely than it might be in the 'ordinary' interactions of daily life.

It can, however, happen that when you move into the second or third days of a retreat, and begin to become aware of the issues that are arising in prayer, you may not like what you see. A natural psychological defence in this situation is to project (or transfer) any negative feelings that are coming up for you onto the person nearest to hand, which will usually be your retreat guide. A sensitive guide will be able to deal with this, and will stay alongside you, uncomplainingly, while you and God explore the painful places. But you yourself might be tempted to decide that this retreat guide is the real cause of the problem, and look for an escape route. If you succeed, and the reason for the discomfort lies with you and your agenda, and not with the guide, then changing to a different guide will not solve anything. Often this kind of problem goes away as the retreat progresses. Through the grace of prayer, the retreatant begins to look more honestly at his or her issues, and stops transferring the negativity to the guide. The guide who seemed like a stumbling block at the beginning of the retreat is often valued as a stepping stone at the end.

So perhaps the advice might be to exercise caution before rejecting a particular guide. Try to express honestly how you feel, and why, and trust that the guide will be able to cope with this. Follow it up with a little patience. See how things go. If there is a genuine impasse, the matter can be referred to the retreat administrator, and sometimes a change can be offered, though this isn't easy to organize without disrupting the retreats of other people.

Above all, let it be a matter for prayer. Sometimes the people who irritate us initially become the grain of sand in our oyster that eventually forms the pearl of great price.

Practicalities

What does a typical retreat cost, and what can I do if I can't afford it?

There is, of course, no such thing as a 'typical retreat', and it follows that any indication of likely cost is merely a very broad guideline of what you might expect.

The range of retreat costs starts at almost nothing and spirals up into thousands of pounds. The best that can be offered here is a guide to the main steps in this range. It needs to be understood that the cost of a retreat depends a great deal on whether the person or organization offering the retreat is doing so as their only means of making a living. When this is the case, the retreatant must expect realistic (but not 'profit-making') charges for the service being offered.

LOW COST RETREATS

The lowest cost retreats are **retreats in daily life**, organized and accompanied by a volunteer **prayer companion/prayer guide**. You can expect to be asked only for a nominal contribution to the expenses of the prayer companions and the cost of hiring the venue (if applicable). On current (2002) prices, this might be as low as £5 per person for a week of guided prayer that is being offered on a local basis. If the prayer companions are travelling from further afield, this cost might increase proportionately. If a public venue is being used for the opening, closing and one-to-one meetings, this too will add to the cost.

Open door retreats are also offered at minimum cost to the retreatant. So are most locally organized **quiet days**, walking retreats and days in **quiet gardens**.

Some centres offer a wonderful range of quiet days, days of reflection, or 'drop-in days' on a donation basis. This means that you will be asked to make a donation within your own means towards the cost of the day. Sometimes a suggested level of donation will be mentioned. A donation, however, is what it says it is. No one will be checking up on what each person has offered. The whole idea is to make access to such days as wide-ranging as possible, so that no one is excluded because they can't afford it.

HIGHER COST RETREATS

Obviously, as soon as accommodation and meals are required, the cost of a retreat goes up. We all know what food, heating, lighting, insurance and all the other costs of running a household amount to today, and every retreat centre carries these costs, as well as the costs of cleaning and household maintenance, often in buildings that are beautiful, old, large, full of atmosphere, but exceedingly expensive to maintain.

On a residential retreat you need to budget for what you would normally expect to pay for bed, breakfast, lunch and evening meal anywhere else. What is actually offered for this price is, however, usually a lot more than you would find in normal holiday accommodation. In an **individually given retreat**, for example, it includes daily sessions with the retreat guide, the daily liturgies, and the invitation to be not so much a guest but a member of the 'family' for the duration of your stay. Again, most retreat centres will invite a suggested offering (though this should not be regarded as 'optional'). On current (2002) prices, this might be around £40 to £45 for each 24-hour period.

Once you have budgeted for the retreat itself, however, there is virtually no other cost, except that of getting there and back. While you are there you will need nothing else – unless, of course, you are a bookworm – most retreat centres run very tempting book stalls!

Some one-day events can also be rather more costly than others. If, for example, a speaker has been invited who is travelling from some distance away, or a more expensive venue is needed, a single day of reflection can sometimes cost up to about £20, or occasionally more, though sometimes concessions are available to those on low incomes.

HELP WITH THE COST OF A RETREAT

As well as offering reductions in price for students, or those on low incomes or state benefits, many retreat houses also have bursary funds available to help people to make a retreat who would not otherwise have the financial means to do so.

These funds are there for you, if you need help. They are there to be used. That is why the money in them has been given. Please do mention any financial strain you may be experiencing to the director or administrator of the retreat house when you apply for a place. It is a straightforward question, and the fact of your asking it will not affect your chance of being offered a retreat place. If there is help available your request will be considered and you will be given a straightforward answer.

The money in bursary funds has been given, over the years, by people who wanted to help others to make a retreat. To the administrator or bursar of a retreat house, responding to a request for financial help is simply a matter of trying to match the resources available to the people who need them at the time. It is not a matter of 'charity', and no one should hesitate to ask for this kind of help.

Do I need to book ahead?

This depends a great deal on where you want to go, and when. Many retreat houses, especially the better known ones, can be booked up *a year in advance*, especially during school holiday periods. Similarly, many smaller retreat centres, with perhaps just a few bedrooms, also fill up quickly.

If a particular **theme retreat** attracts you, it is wise to make up your mind quickly and phone through to the retreat centre to enquire about a place. Usually a centre will accept a phone booking, if it is followed up within the next few days with a written confirmation and deposit. Some retreat centres have web sites, that will indicate the current availability of retreat places, but don't rely too heavily on these. Better, usually, to check personally, by phone or by letter. And if you do make a written enquiry, please enclose a stamped self-addressed envelope for the reply.

Theme retreats tend to be advertised in advance in the publicity brochures for the retreat centre, usually issued each year, or sometimes every six months. Many of them are also listed in the *Retreats* magazine.

Retreats in daily life are usually only advertised locally, around the centre where they are being held (parish, school, college, etc.). Because of the nature of a daily life retreat, it is not so crucial to book ahead, because usually extra people can be welcomed by inviting extra **prayer companions/prayer guides** to join the retreat.

If you have set your heart on making an **individually given retreat** in a particular retreat centre, do contact the centre as soon as you are able to give definite dates. Many people are disappointed every year, because they have left it too late to join the retreat of their choice. Most retreat centres, however, also hold waiting lists and because of the long lead time between booking and actually making the retreat, there is a reasonable chance of being offered a place if you are near the top of the waiting list.

Will there be daily worship?

This depends very much on the custom of the individual retreat centre. In some of the larger centres a daily Eucharist is celebrated and is felt to be a pivotal point in the day. Often a time for silent shared prayer is also set aside, either in the morning or evening.

Where daily acts of worship are celebrated, they are optional. However, almost everyone who makes a retreat finds themselves drawn to share in worship with the other retreatants and with the community living in the house. For some the opportunity for regular worship (which may include attendance at the daily office in a religious community) turns out to be a quite unexpected joy. For others the freedom to opt out of formal worship is valued.

In smaller centres a daily Eucharist may not be possible, but an opportunity for shared prayer usually will be, and there will always be a chapel or similar room where all can gather for prayer.

In an **individually given retreat**, these oases of shared worship are an opportunity for the individual retreatants to come together in prayer, reminding each of us that we are part of a much greater 'Whole'.

In a **theme retreat**, the retreat leader will often suggest a time of shared prayer or morning or evening praise and worship. Sometimes these times will be silent and contemplative. Sometimes they will be vocal and exuberant. This depends a great deal on the Christian tradition(s) of those who are there. Two of my loveliest memories, for example, are of a day of reflection in the East End of London, among a mix, mainly, of Cockney and Caribbean men and women, who broke into song quite spontaneously at one point in our prayer, and of a retreat in Dublin, when the Sunday Mass was wonderfully enlivened by the magical harmonies of traditional prayers sung by the retreatants in the Irish language.

If you are making a residential retreat, where a daily Eucharist or other form of worship is celebrated, your retreat guide may well ask you to contribute to that worship on one or more of your days there. You may be invited to read, for example, or to bring up the offertory gifts, or to serve as a eucharistic minister. You are free, of course, to say 'No', but don't let your nervousness take over: to share in this way is a way of ministering to your fellow retreatants, and is nothing like as threatening as it may at first appear.

If daily worship is an important factor in your choice of a retreat, it is worth asking beforehand what the house arrangements are.

Will there be time out to relax?

In any retreat, the hoped-for encounter with God and with our deepest and truest self, happens most readily when we are relaxed and receptive, free of preconceptions about God, God's will and our own 'performance'. So 'relaxation' is built into the process.

First, relaxation in our approach to prayer – letting God be God to us and in us, rather than trying to 'achieve' some kind of 'success' in prayer. And second, relaxation from our normal, often stressful, daily schedules.

The shape and form of this second kind of relaxation during a retreat depends on the type and the duration of the retreat.

Most people sign up for a one-day event, a quiet day or theme day, because they are looking for some nourishment in their spiritual life, and they will often be looking to the **retreat guide** to provide it. A good retreat leader, however, will remain always aware that it is God alone who offers this longed-for nourishment. He or she will only offer a focus for the search for that nourishment – a few pointers to help the retreatants bring their hearts and minds to rest in a particular direction. Then time will be set aside for each retreatant to reflect on what has been offered, and let God speak to them as individuals. This is the time to 'relax' and listen to God, perhaps by walking round the garden, or sitting beside the window or the lake, or simply closing our eyes, and resting in the peace of the place of 'oasis'. It would be reasonable to expect at least a couple of hours during a quiet day for this kind of 'time out'.

In a longer **theme retreat**, this kind of pattern will recur day by day. Sometimes evening activities might be arranged, purely for relaxation purposes – maybe a time for being together socially with the other retreatants. Some retreatants report that they valued the free time very highly and would have liked more of it. Others actually find it unexpectedly difficult to 'relax' and to fill in the available leisure time fruitfully. And certainly some theme retreats are more structured and 'full' than others. If you know in advance that you are looking for a more structured form of retreat, it is worth asking the organizers for a little more detail about the shape of the days before you finally book a place.

In an **individually given retreat**, the nature of time out for relaxation will be for each retreatant to define for themselves. It is wise to allow time each day for pure recreation, during which you feel free to follow your nose, with no conscious attempt to 'pray' or 'reflect' – though in fact, as you will discover, the reflective process is a continuous one, which will be enhanced and enriched by your taking time simply to 'be'.

You may feel the desire to fill up your 'free time' in an individually given retreat by reading books. If so, talk the matter through with your retreat guide. Reading (even 'spiritual reading') can very easily become a serious distraction from whatever God is wanting to open up with you in your prayer, and it sometimes offers us an unconscious 'excuse' to avoid things within us that we could be looking at in prayer. Reading might therefore not be a good way to relax on retreat, because the theme of the book will unconsciously soak through into your prayer and reflection, and may deflect it. The same thing applies to writing letters, or making lengthy phone calls, or watching television. All have the potential to distract in a negative way. Your retreat guide will help you to discern what might be helpful to you and what might be a distraction. Physical exercise, however, especially if it involves walking in a garden, in the countryside, or along the seashore, can be both relaxing, and conducive to reflection.

In a really long silent retreat (more than eight days) definite rest, or repose, days will be scheduled, when you will be free to take yourself off for the day if you wish, and possibly to talk with other retreatants.

What is the optimum length of time to spend in retreat?

How long is a piece of string?

The answer to this question depends entirely upon the person making the retreat and the particular needs of that person at the time.

Nevertheless, a silent retreat does have a certain dynamic, and the typical five, six or eight day duration reflects something of this dynamic. People often find that it can take two or three days to settle into retreat. It is surprisingly difficult to 'switch off' to all that was going on in our normal daily life before we came away on retreat. The first couple of days are the time for winding down, and, for many people, for catching up on much needed rest and relaxation. During these first days, a retreatant may well be over-concerned with 'What am I going to make of this retreat? What is its shape going to be?' Only when we stop worrying about questions like these does God get a word in edgeways, and the real issues begin to emerge.

The third, fourth and fifth days can be the time when these issues come up in prayer and in your conversations with the guide. There can also be a bit of a trough around the third or fourth day, especially if the retreat doesn't seem to be 'going anywhere' in a way that the retreatant can readily recognize. Prayer too, when it is intensive, as in an individually given retreat, claims energy, and a certain spiritual exhaustion can show itself, if the retreatant is not pacing him or herself. (For more guidance on this, see Part III.) The last day or two should be focused on the gradual gathering of the fruits of the retreat, and preparation for the return home.

So, for an **individually given retreat**, in which you are seeking to be open before God about serious issues in your life, at least five or six days would be recommended, and eight would give rather more space, of course. For a **theme retreat**, the purpose of which is to nourish you and encourage you along your journey, the optimum time is whatever time you can spare. A weekend is fine. A week is fine too.

Is making a retreat rather a spartan experience?

If we look back into history, and reflect on how, for example, the early monks 'retreated', or how Jesus himself withdrew into the hills, often without food or water, to come closer to the Father, we might well ask ourselves how so many of our modern retreat houses come to be so comfortable.

But retreat houses, like most other things, come in all styles and degrees of comfort. Probably the most significant factor that makes us feel at ease in a retreat house has less to do with the physical comforts it offers, than with the atmosphere of warmth and acceptance that prevails there.

However, it is true that most retreat houses are warm and comfortable, both physically and psychologically. The nearest you will get to 'asceticism' is a certain simplicity. A 'simply appointed' retreat house will provide you with a (probably quite small) bedroom, usually with its own wash basin and towel rail, a small cupboard where you can hang your clothes, maybe a bookshelf, a chair and a little desk or writing area. Toilet and shower facilities will usually be close by, and shared with several other retreatants. Meals will be simple, but satisfying and varied, often set out for you to serve yourself. You may well be expected to help with some of the work of the house, including clearing tables, washing up and, certainly, stripping and remaking your bed when you leave.

At the other end of the 'comfort scale', some retreat houses will offer you a spacious room, sometimes with en suite facilities, and more food than you could possibly eat. There may be other luxuries too, such as a jacuzzi, massage, aromatherapy, reflexology, and so on.

Unless stated otherwise, you can expect to enjoy the privacy of a single room. The *Retreats* listings include details of the nature of the accommodation in this respect.

Is fasting part of the process of making a retreat?

The subject of fasting as a spiritual exercise is beyond the scope of this book. Suffice it to say that no retreat house would ever assume that you are intending to fast, while on retreat, though some retreatants do want to do so, at least for part of the time. Sometimes this intention fades when they see the provisions on offer, and indeed, offering hospitality is an important part of the ministry of retreat-giving. The house offers the hospitality of a warm welcome and a comfortable place to sleep and eat, and enjoy recreation. The **retreat guide** offers the hospitality of a listening heart and a place where you can be truly yourself without fear of disapproval or diminishment. These are ways in which we can reveal God's love to each other. So you might like to think twice before entering into a strict fast while on retreat.

If you do decide to miss one or more meals throughout your retreat, all you need to do is let the house administrator know in advance, to avoid the wastage of food. There may be a list that you can tick each day if you don't require a particular meal. Vegetarian options are offered by most retreat centres. Take care before entering upon a strict fast, either in retreat or out of it, and seek medical advice as appropriate.

I'm a night owl. Will I be expected to get up at the crack of dawn, or to be in bed by 10 o'clock?

Thankfully, the kingdom of heaven has plenty of mansions – room for the night owls and the early birds and all variations in between. And while a retreat house isn't exactly the kingdom of heaven, it does – or should – try at least to operate on the same lines!

So, in a typical residential retreat, either a **theme retreat** or an **individually given retreat**, your days and nights will be yours to dispose more or less as you will. Within the constraints of set meal times and the timing of any teaching sessions you may be attending, or meetings with your **retreat guide**, you will be free to set your own timetable, and to vary it as you wish.

The only restriction on this overall freedom is that you avoid disturbing anyone else. Get up at 6 a.m. if you wish, but don't wake the neighbours. Stay up until the wee small hours, but observe the quiet of the night that will certainly prevail in the house after 10 p.m. Most retreat houses have facilities for making yourself a hot drink at any time of the day or night. And it is perfectly possible to do so without disturbing the night peace, just as it is possible to wander around and maybe use the chapel or other places for prayer, or simply to relieve your insomnia. When you are on retreat, you are simply living in a rather bigger family than usual and the same guidelines of courteous consideration apply. Many people on retreat do choose to take part in whatever services are celebrated by the community of the house, and find that this enriches their own re-treat. But such attendance is optional, and no one will be watching your every move to check on whether you are going or not. Every-one will respect your personal freedom to choose.

However, if you are making a retreat in a religious house where you have chosen to participate in the daily life of the order itself, you will of course be expected to attend the daily office or other ser-vices that shape the day of the community. In this situation there will be a more strict delineation of night and day, and you will be told the necessary arrangements and details of timing at the begin-ning of your retreat.

It sometimes happens that people find the experience of being in retreat alters familiar sleep patterns – usually for the better. Habitual late 'owls' may discover, to their benefit, that the hours before midnight may also be slept in. Habitual late risers may come to know that the joy of daybreak is sometimes worth waking up for, while overtired 7 o'clock starters relish the extra hour or two under the duvet. All things are possible with God, especially in retreat!

PART III
Before, During and After

Preparing for your retreat

A retreat is a special time. It is an appointment with the deepest part of yourself, where God is indwelling. You will probably be thinking about it for weeks ahead of the actual date. As for a holiday, but even more so, you will be making preparations in your head, and in your heart. In this section we will have a look at a few things you might like to consider, in your thinking ahead.

Practical preparations

If you are planning to make a retreat in daily life, your plans may need to take account of the following questions:

- Are you familiar with the way such a retreat is usually run? If not, you might like to read through the entries headed **Retreats in daily life** and **Prayer companion/prayer guide**, in Section IV. These will give you some idea of what to expect from your retreat, and of the role of your companion.
- Are you familiar with the venue for the opening meeting of the retreat? Have you set aside the time to go to it?
- Have you made whatever arrangements are necessary to allow you to be free to meet with your prayer companion on a regular basis? The exact timings and frequency will be decided at the opening meeting, and most prayer companions are prepared to be fairly flexible, though remember that they too will often have to arrange themselves around the needs of their own work and family.

If you are planning to make a residential retreat, your practical preparations may be rather more extensive:

- If you have family commitments, have you made arrangements for someone to look after children/elderly or infirm relatives/pets while you are away from home?
- Do you know what to expect when you arrive at the location of your retreat? If not, read through the entries headed **Theme**

retreats, Individually given retreats, Retreat guide/retreat director and **Daily routine on retreat** for further information.

- Do you know what time to arrive, and what you need to take with you? The retreat house will normally give you information about arrival and departure times well in advance. If you are unsure, just give the retreat house a call to check. Some suggestions are offered below as to what to take with you.
- Have you notified the retreat house of any special requirements you may have? For example, wheelchair access or other mobility needs (such as a room on the ground floor, or easy access to a bathroom), any dietary needs, loop system availability for the hard of hearing, especially during a theme retreat when it is important to be able to hear the speaker.

What will you need on retreat?

For a daily life retreat, very little will be needed. It is a good idea to have a Bible with you at each meeting with your guide, and to keep a notebook and pencil handy throughout the retreat, to make a note of the guide's suggestions for prayer, and for any thoughts, feelings or reflections you may wish to share with your guide at your next meeting.

For any residential retreat the following checklist may be helpful (though it is by no means exhaustive):

- Casual, comfortable clothes that you feel really 'at home' in. There's no need to take half the wardrobe with you, but it is important that you feel at ease in whatever you *do* take.
- Sandals or comfortable indoor shoes, for use in the house.
- Strong, outdoor shoes, or walking boots, if the retreat house is situated in an area where it is possible to go for country or seaside walks. If in doubt, err on the side of assuming that you will need these. It can be very disappointing to arrive in a place where the great outdoors is beckoning you, but you have no suitable shoes in which to explore it.
- Warm, weatherproof outdoor clothing, if you are hoping to go for walks.

- Personal toiletries, including towels (if these are not provided. If you are in doubt about this, check before you go).
- A Bible, notebook and pens/pencils.
- Optionally, colouring pencils and a drawing pad.
- Any objects that you would like to have with you as aids to meditation. Note, however, that the use of candles may not be permitted, because of the fire risk. Please check with the retreat house administration before you use candles in your room.
- An alarm clock. This may sound like the last thing you think you want with you on retreat, but it can be helpful to know that if you want to be awake in time for breakfast, morning prayer, an early meeting with your guide, you won't miss it by oversleeping. You don't have to set it, of course, if you don't need to, but just knowing that it is there may actually help you to sleep better.

AND A FEW THINGS YOU WON'T BE NEEDING

Books. It can be quite a serious distraction (especially during an individually given retreat) to read books, because these can seriously deflect you from the path God is inviting you to walk with him. However, I personally always take some poetry with me, to relax with out in the garden when the sun shines or to ponder before falling asleep. If you must read, try to do so only for the purpose of relaxation, and don't be tempted to use your retreat as a time to study some aspect of theology, or the latest offering from some spiritual guru, or whatever else. Give the time to God and trust God to use it wisely and in your own best interest.

Elaborate clothes. You won't be going to any dinner parties, or dining at the captain's table. Just take what you feel easy in. Travelling light can be a spiritual statement, as well as an easier way to make a journey.

High tech accessories, such as your laptop computer, your radio cassette player or your mobile phone. As with all things, the exception proves the rule of course. You may find, for example, that your Walkman helps you to relax, if you use it to listen to your favourite gentle music. Or you may feel you need a mobile if there is an urgent need to contact home (though most retreat houses will have a payphone), but if you have it with you, do keep it switched off when not in use, for your own sake and for the sake of your fellow retreatants. Try, as far as you possibly can, to leave all traces and reminders of your work behind you when you set off to your retreat, and *insist* that your work leaves *you* alone for the duration. And in a silent retreat, try to experience the silence as fully as you can.

Personal preparations

The way an individual prepares for a retreat is a very personal matter, but a few things can be mentioned that may be more generally helpful.

If you are going to make a **retreat in daily life**, the most important piece of preparation might be to reflect on *how*, and *where*, and *when* you are hoping to make your regular time of prayer. Your day may already be so busy that it isn't yet clear how you are going to make time for prayer, but the value of your retreat will be diminished if you can't take time for prayer in a fairly deliberate way, if not every day, then at least three or four times during the week. Some guidelines for this process are offered later on in this section, but as a preparation you might like to consider:

- *How much time you can give to prayer* each day, or on a regular basis. Do be realistic! Ten minutes time alone in prayer, faithfully adhered to day by day, is much more effective than high hopes of half an hour a day that you almost never manage, and as a result feel discontented with yourself, making you much more likely to give up the whole thing.
- *Where you can go to pray.* Prayer time, ideally, needs to be in a place where you can be alone and uninterrupted for as long as you have decided to set aside. In the midst of family life this can be difficult. Some people choose to go out to a nearby park, or into a church, for their prayer time. Others find it possible to switch off and focus on God while they are making their commuter journey by bus or train. You may be able to find a few quiet moments in your own home, perhaps in the early morning, or after the children have gone to school, or to bed. If so, can you choose a definite place in the house that is to be 'your space'? Maybe keep a candle there, with your Bible, or some token of your desire to

pray. Have a comfortable chair there – preferably one that is straight-backed and supportive, but also welcoming. A prayer cushion or prayer stool is a good alternative. Having a special place like this will help you to move more readily into a relaxed and prayerful state of mind, and will help your time of prayer to become a daily joy.

- *What time of day best suits your routine.* Some people are natural larks and others are nightingales. Many find that a time of prayer in the early morning, before the rest of the household is awake, is pure gift, setting the whole day off to a good start. For others the very idea of rising at 6 a.m. is a nightmare. Listen to your own body clock, and try to find a time when you are alert, but able to relax for the time you have allocated to prayer. Night prayer is a lovely habit to form, but it may also be a time when you regularly fall asleep in the middle of your meditation. Remember, too, that prayer can permeate your whole day, consciously and unconsciously. More guidance on keeping prayer alive in this way is offered later in this section.

These same guidelines also apply if you are planning to make a residential retreat. Your guide will help you to organize your day in retreat, incorporating prayer, reflection, rest and exercise in a balanced way. Because there are no other distractions, you will probably find it much easier to make space and time for prayer, and as regards the place for prayer, you will be spoiled for choice – your own room, the chapel(s) and quiet room(s) in the house and the countryside outside the doors.

Whatever type of retreat you are making, you might also like to spend a little time before it begins, just reflecting on these questions:

- *What am I bringing with me into this retreat?* Just let yourself become aware of any issues that are around in your life right now, either positive or negative. Don't try to resolve them, and don't make judgements about them. Just let them be there in your awareness. Don't assume that the retreat will centre on these issues – God may have quite other plans for his time with you in retreat – but simply to be aware of what you are carrying by way of baggage may help to clear the pathways a little for the journey of prayer that lies ahead of you.

- *What am I actually hoping for from this retreat?* What is my desire? If God were to ask me: 'What would you most like me to do for you right now?' how would I answer? It is good to be aware of what your heart is desiring (however unlikely you think its fulfilment may be!). Simply carry these desires into your prayer, and into your retreat, and if you feel you wish to do so, share them with your prayer companion.

The most helpful piece of advice I was ever given, regarding prayer in retreat, was just before I left home to go on my first residential retreat. The advice was this:

'No predictions!'

Making the most of your retreat

The day has arrived, and your retreat is beginning. Whether it comprises just a single day of quiet, reflective time, or several days, or even weeks, in solitude, whether it is happening amid the stress of everyday life, or in the seclusion of a retreat house, you will want it to be as fruitful as it possibly can be, and a source of nourishment for a long time to come.

How can you help this to happen, given that prayer is gift, and not something any of us can 'achieve'? We might look at a few ways of making your day(s) of quiet as rich in blessing as possible.

Stop worrying

Whenever I make a journey, I find myself going over and over in my mind all the things I may have forgotten. This usually carries on until I have passed the halfway mark of the journey, and realized that whatever I have forgotten, it is not now going to be worth going back for it. I can then focus my attention on what lies ahead rather than what I have left behind.

In a retreat, you will be leaving quite a lot behind. In a residential retreat, this will include your work, your family, your friends, your duties and the expectations that others impose upon you. A rare treat, and one that will not last for ever, so make the most of it. Your job, believe it or not, will continue to be done in your absence, and your family will continue to be fed. You have made all the necessary arrangements, so now is the time to enjoy the freedom. In a retreat in daily life, this sense of freedom comes in smaller packages: the time you have given over to prayer each day, and the time for meeting your guide, but these times, too, are 'freedom times', just for you and God to share.

To 'stop worrying' is much easier to say than to do, but nevertheless, once your retreat has begun, there is nothing more you can do to ensure that life continues while you are away. This is the first hurdle of trust. Of course, if real anxieties or emergencies should arise during your retreat, you will need to attend to them, but you will not be on your own. Your retreat guide and other members of the retreat house community will do everything they possibly can to help you resolve whatever needs to be resolved. Problems in the boardroom or on the shop floor, and routine family squabbles, should *not*, however, be allowed to count as 'emergencies'!

Finding and maintaining the best routine

While you were still planning your retreat, you may have worked out just how and when you were intending to make the time for prayer and reflection. During a **quiet day** or a quiet weekend, this will, generally, be fixed for you. The retreat leader will have planned in some time for quiet, private prayer, and in this case simply use the time to focus on anything that particularly spoke to you during the preceding talk, and let your prayer lead you where it will.

In a **retreat in daily life**, be continually aware, day by day, of the intention you originally formed regarding how long to pray each day. The length of time is less important than the discipline of staying faithful to what you decide on. Often prayer 'comes alive' at the end of a period set aside for it. If you get bored halfway through and cut the time short, you may be missing the very grace you are praying for. To be faithful to the time we are giving to God in prayer is also a way of embodying our real desire to deepen our relationship with him.

If you find that your original hopes about when and where to make your prayer time are not working out in practice, it might be worth sitting back quietly and reviewing the situation, possibly talking it through with your prayer companion, and making changes if necessary. It may also be worth reflecting on the *reasons* why what you intended isn't really happening. Sometimes there are objective reasons – practical matters that we can do little to change. If this is the case, then try to work around them in settling on a more helpful time and place for prayer. On the other hand, sometimes our reluctance to make a definite time for prayer lies in ourselves, because we are unconsciously shying away from what we think the silence may uncover. If you sense that this may be the case, the need to honour the time you have decided on is especially important, and it may also be helpful to talk through these feelings with your **prayer companion/prayer guide**.

In a residential retreat, there is a need to give some structure to your days. In a **theme retreat**, this structure will usually be imposed by the timing of the input or teaching sessions. In an **individually given retreat**, the structure of the day is largely yours to determine. A general guide is given in Part IV under **Daily routine on retreat**. Your retreat guide will be able to help you plan for prayer times during the day, if you wish it.

You will certainly benefit most from your time in retreat if you can establish a balance in your days between the following aspects:

- Periods of 'deliberate' prayer
- Reflection on your prayer
- Relaxation
- Exercise
- Shared prayer or worship with the other retreatants and/or the community

Engaging with the created world

Your retreat should be an experience of wholeness, which includes a retreat for your body as well as for your mind and soul. The retreat house will look after your need for good nourishment, and will probably offer suggestions about walks and rambles beyond the retreat house grounds. It is up to you to make the exercise happen, and – above all – to *enjoy* it. These days in retreat are a rare opportunity to really engage with the created world around you. There is time for whatever you want to do. I know of someone who went for a walk along a country lane during a retreat, and stopped to gaze at the life going on in a tree at the roadside. Who knows how long he had been standing there, reflecting on all he was seeing, before he became aware that a car was waiting patiently to get past him on the narrow road.

So, without causing traffic jams, take this God-given opportunity to notice what is happening, moment by moment, among God's other creatures, gradually reconnecting to the deeper wholeness underlying all our apparent separateness. Use all your senses. Notice and engage with all the different shifts in the weather, the changing patterns of cloud, the movements of the wind, the varying shades of light throughout the day, the clarity of the stars, the phases of the moon. You will be surprised how deeply God can speak to your heart through the simple awareness of the living world. I personally find that a reflective walk like this each day is an invaluable part of a retreat, as well as being a simple delight for its own sake. If walking isn't easy, or the weather is less than friendly, spend some time at your window, letting the view enter your soul and speak its meanings to you.

During a **retreat in daily life**, too, it is well worth taking just a little extra time at some point during each day, simply to be present to the created world. A walk down the garden, or a few minutes in the park can help to restore perspective in a stressful daily routine. A few moments gazing at your sleeping child, or sitting with an elderly relative. Time just to be with your cat or dog, and appreciate all that makes them so wonderfully 'other'. Time to arrange a few flowers more purposefully than usual, or to reflect on what you are really doing when you prepare the family meal. Five minutes away from the office, to walk round the car park. Maybe an extra effort to spend quality time with a friend, a partner, or your children – a relaxing hour in the pub or a special meal can be just as much a part of your retreat in daily life as the time you have set yourself for prayer, because these things are all drawing your focus beyond the boundaries of your own 'kingdom' to the ways in which God is to be discovered in the world around you.

How will I pray?

Everyone who is seeking God will have their own way of prayer. Use whatever approach to prayer you find most helpful, and 'pray as you can, not as you can't'. It may be, however, that during a time of retreat, new ways of prayer offer themselves, or you may feel drawn to pray in ways you haven't tried before. Talk to your guide about new approaches to prayer, if this is part of what you are looking for. Your guide may suggest new possibilities, not because there is anything wrong with how you normally pray, but simply to open up new doors for you, that you may or may not choose to go through. A time of retreat can be an ideal opportunity for exploring the possibilities of, for example, imaginative meditation, or praying with scripture. Some suggestions for further reading on the subject of prayer are included at the end of this book.

Reflecting on your prayer

An essential component of 'prayer', especially during retreat, is the reflection *after* a period of prayer on how you were feeling *during* the prayer, what movements you noticed within yourself, what the prayer seemed to be about, and where it might be leading.

All too often in normal daily life, there is precious little time for prayer in itself, let alone for reflecting on the effects of that prayer, but in retreat things are different. There *is* time. You have cleared some space in your life to *make* time. Whether you are making your retreat in daily life or in seclusion, the importance of this kind of reflection cannot be overstated. It is a way of gathering the fruits of a time of prayer, and incorporating them into your life.

The purpose of this kind of reflection is to increase your awareness of the ways in which God is active in your life, and of your own response to that activity. Things to notice during a period of reflection might include:

- *How did I feel during this time of prayer?* Could I say that I was, as it were, in harmony with myself and with God, in a kind of inner resonance with my true self, or was I feeling disturbed, uncomfortable, distracted? Was I 'tuned in to the core of my being', or was there a lot of interference? Did the time pass quickly, or was I struggling to 'stay with it'? Whatever you notice, in your reflection, don't make any judgements about it. Simply be aware of it, and maybe share your reactions with your **prayer companion**. These different nuances of feeling during a time of prayer, followed by some reflection on what may have been the root cause of those feelings, can be a help in discerning what is drawing you closer to God and what is tending to pull you further away.

- *Did anything particularly strike me in what I was using as a focus for my prayer* (perhaps a passage of scripture, or an imaginative contemplation of a Gospel scene, or a look back over the events and reactions of the past day)? Just notice anything that caused a reaction in you, whether that reaction was positive or negative. A strong reaction is a sign that your psyche (where the Holy Spirit is indwelling) is signalling interest in something, and nudging you with an invitation to look at this point more deeply, perhaps taking it back into your next period of prayer.

- *Are there any connections to be made between what has arisen in my prayer and what is happening in my life, or in the life of the world I live in?* One of the most potent gifts, especially of scriptural prayer, is to lead us to discover connections between the actions and values of God and the events and demands of our own daily lives. When we start to make these connections, and live out their consequences, then prayer really starts to make a difference.

- *Did the prayer leave me enlightened or challenged in any particular way?* Be specific, and maybe make a note of what you find. A feeling of discomfort around some issue, for example, may be an invitation from God to make some necessary change of attitude or action. A period of prayer that has been experienced as deeply peaceful may have opened up new perspectives and insights for you, or helped you to deepen your awareness that you truly are a loved child of God and a cherished part of God's creation.

- *What was the one most significant aspect of the prayer?* For what gift, granted in the prayer, do I most wish to thank God for? Is there one thing I would like to go back to?

- *What do I want to share with my prayer companion from this period of prayer?* Again, make a note of any points that you want to bring up at the next meeting with your guide. This helps in two ways: it encourages you to *focus* on what was really most significant for you in the prayer; and it helps you to make the best use of the time with your guide.

Pacing yourself

A retreat can be a much longed for time of withdrawal, bringing with it the temptation to 'pack in' as much prayer as humanly possible. This temptation may need to be resisted. The longer the period of retreat, the greater the need to 'pace' yourself, to avoid spiritual and physical exhaustion. A weekend retreat may well be something of a fast sprint, but an eight-day retreat is more like a middle-distance run, while a 30-day retreat is definitely a marathon. If you try to run a middle-distance race at the speed of a fast sprint, the results will disappoint you, as every athlete knows. Take time to relax and to reflect and to keep a balance in your days.

Making the most of your meetings with the companion/guide

If you are making an **individually given retreat**, whether in seclusion or in daily life, you will be meeting your retreat guide on a regular basis, for the duration of the retreat. These meetings are invaluable opportunities to grow in your discernment of what God is doing in your life, and where God is calling you to be. The following guidelines may help you to ensure that these meetings are as fruitful as possible:

- *Do be punctual in arriving at the meeting.* Your guide may well be seeing several other retreatants, and will be relying on your respecting the time schedules involved. If you are unable to attend one of the meetings with a guide during a **retreat in daily life**, please try to get a message through beforehand, so that the guide can replan as necessary.
- *Prepare yourself a little beforehand*, by going through any notes you have made during your periods of reflection since you last met

with the guide. The more you are able to focus on what really matters to you most, the less likely you are to get to the end of the meeting without having said what you really needed to say.

- *Be as open as possible with your guide, to the extent that you feel safe to be so.* Your guide will be attempting to be alongside you, helping you to discern where God has been especially present to you and what this presence is meaning for you. Guides are not mind-readers, though they should be able to read body language. Tell it like it is, not as you think the guide (or God!) would like it to be. The guide may say very little during the meeting. This isn't a sign of lack of interest, but an indication of good, non-intrusive companionship. Listen to whatever the guide does have to say, which will usually be at the end of the meeting, and take on board anything that 'rings true' with you.

- *Try to retain a feeling for the passage of time during the meeting.* It is the responsibility of the guide to keep the meeting to the set time, but you can help by not leaving the most important issues until the last five minutes. Remember that the guide will probably have another appointment following on from your meeting and if your meeting overruns, someone else will be getting short measure.

Sleeping, dreaming

If you are making a residential retreat, this may be a rare opportunity to catch up on some sleep, and even to break a poor sleep pattern. You are on retreat. It's OK to sleep longer in the morning if you wish, to have an afternoon nap, to go to bed as early or as late as you wish. Many retreat guides will positively encourage you to wind down and rest for the first couple of days of a retreat. Prayer does not come easily to the person who is exhausted, and very many people come into retreat in a seriously exhausted state.

We hear God's word in our hearts, and feel his touch upon our lives most readily when we are rested, relaxed and receptive. Sometimes he needs to 'switch us off' so as to get his word in edgeways. Indeed I have come across people who have been struggling for years to deal with some problem in their lives, and a whole new perspective has opened up when they were 'off guard', or even fast asleep! Which brings us to dreams. You may dream more in retreat, or rather, you may be more mindful of your dreams. Notice them, and share them with your guide if you wish to do so. They may be another way in which God is speaking within you. They can sometimes be extensions of your waking prayer.

Expect the unexpected

Finally, start each new day of your retreat with hopeful expectancy, but without any predictions. You might like to begin each morning with a short time of prayer on waking, committing the day and all its surprises to God, asking God to direct every particle of your being towards himself, and giving back to him the minutes and hours of the day to use as he will to deepen your relationship with him.

Keeping the retreat experience alive

You may well have arrived at the beginning of your retreat with feelings of trepidation, but the chances are that when your retreat comes to an end – a day, a weekend, six, eight, or even 30 days later – you will have very mixed feelings about going back to the everyday life you have temporarily withdrawn from. A common reaction to a period of retreat is simply to wish that it could continue for much longer.

Time in retreat can never be a permanent dwelling place but is more like a stay at an oasis. The whole point of the oasis is to provide rest, refreshment, life-giving water and time for reflection, in order to give new perspective, purpose and energy to the ongoing journey. How might these gifts be carried back to the world of everyday, in ways that make a difference to that ongoing journey?

Each retreat will yield its own fruits, and only the individual retreatant can discover what, exactly, has been given for the journey ahead, and how this gift is to become embodied in real life choices and decisions. However, there are some general principles that can help us to move on – bearing in mind that after a retreat we are not going *back*, to where we came from, but going *forward* to a new stage in our journeying.

Keeping prayer alive

During your retreat you will have been making time for prayer in ways that seem impossible amid the stress of daily living. Your days of retreat have, in some form or another, been totally focused on your relationship with God. Whether your prayer has been made in formal ways, at fixed times, or while you were strolling through the gardens, or gazing at the view, or simply being wholly present to the present moment, your hours in retreat have been, as it were, woven out of prayer. Going home can seem like a painful break in this pattern. There is absolutely no chance of keeping prayer alive in that kind of way, you may feel.

And you would be right! Tomorrow you return to the demands of job and family, neighbours and community. Prayer will have to find its space in all of that. When I sense the hopelessness of 'staying close to God' as I return from retreat, it helps me to reflect on the pattern of Jesus' own living. I find him, in the Gospel accounts, regularly taking time out to be with the Father in prayer, in a quiet place. But I also find him, for the most part, in the thick of daily life, with crowds clamouring on all sides, begging for his touch, arguing with his position, listening, debating, demanding.

So it seems to me, from this model, that prayer has these two faces: a small amount of time in solitude, wholly focused on the Father, and a very large amount of time spent in the bustle of the market place, living out what has been discovered in the time of silent solitude. Why would we expect the pattern of our own Christian living to be any other than this? Looked at in this way, the time we spend simply responding to the demands of daily life (which may well be over 95 per cent of our waking hours) is not a time that cuts us off from prayer, but a time when the fruits of prayer are becoming incarnate in our lives – translated into real choices and real action for a real world. We may well not recognize this process in ourselves, but in reality the time we spend in prayer is quietly bearing kingdom fruit.

So perhaps it is important to honour both aspects of the reality of prayer in this way: to make time for some silence and solitude, some time alone with God, and then to let the fruits of that time spill over into everything we do. In practical terms, we might approach this challenge in two ways:

- By deliberately choosing to arrange our lives around some still centre of prayer. It is important to be realistic about this, and better to plan to spend ten minutes in prayer each day, and actually do so, than to plan for an hour a day, and become frustrated with ourselves because we 'fail'.
- By then getting on with the day, dealing with everything that it presents us with, but seeking to grow in *awareness* of the many ways in which our time with God is shaping and affecting our minute-by-minute reactions and decisions. We might call this the need for *ongoing reflection*.

Bear in mind, too, that prayer can be a continual process, simply in the daily awareness of God's presence in all we experience. There are many more ways to pray than during our 'official' prayer time. A few possibilities for discovering more expansive and flexible forms of prayer are suggested in some of the books listed under 'Suggestions for further reading' at the end of this book.

Living reflectively

We can get in touch with this dynamic process of reflection if we take a few moments each day just to call to mind what has been happening during the day. A few minutes in the evening doing this kind of exercise can make a huge difference to the ways in which our prayer becomes effective in our living. Everyone will find their own way of doing this reflection, but the following questions may be helpful:

- When I 're-spool' the story of the day, what jumps out at me as being especially significant? Both good and bad memories of the day's events may come to mind. Both are equally important, as potential pointers towards God's action in our lives.
- How did I react to these events or interactions? With hindsight,

which of my reactions were coming from the deepest, truest part of myself, and which reactions came from a feeling of being 'driven', perhaps by my own fears or more superficial desires, or perhaps by the will of other people?

- Are there any inadequate reactions that I want to acknowledge, and bring to God for healing? Is there any unfinished business that I want to commit to God? Is there anything I feel prompted to do or to say tomorrow to help correct my course, or to heal an injury I may have caused?

- What was the best thing that happened today? How do I want to express my gratitude for it? How might I share it, so that others may have a part in its life-giving quality?

- Where was my prayer especially focused today? What has happened during the day that has 'connected' to the hopes, desires or dreams that shaped my prayer? Sometimes we simply don't notice the subtle ways in which God has answered prayer, because we don't give ourselves time to reflect in this way.

Gradually this kind of reflection will become a habit. Eventually it will pervade all we do, so that a period of reflective prayer turns into a continuous state of reflective living.

Taking time to be

The experience of retreat was an invitation to *wholeness*. It was easy, in the seclusion of the retreat setting, to become more aware of what helps to make us whole. And when we go home it can feel as though all trace of that 'wholeness' has fragmented again, leaving us struggling to keep all the bits and pieces of our lives somehow 'together'. Yet it needn't be so. There are many ways that we can explore in our daily living that can draw us back into a wholeness of body, mind and spirit. If we can build some of these ways into our everyday routine, it will become easier to nourish the awareness and reflectiveness that leads us to the core of our being. A few examples might be:

- *Take a little time, regularly, to reconnect to the natural world around you.* Just a five-minute walk down the garden, or along the road to the post box, or a few minutes in silence looking at the view beyond the window, watching the sun set, listening to the rain falling, letting yourself be in awe of the storm, or the wind, or the gathering clouds. In retreat, this kind of relationship with creation became almost second nature. There is no need to lose touch with it now you are home.

- *Choose something that helps you to relax, and build it into your weekly routine.* Maybe you enjoy music: if so, choose your favourite CD and listen to it, with your full attention. If you enjoy reading, treat yourself to a book you haven't read, maybe once a month, and give yourself the gift of some time each week to read it. If your choice is a more active one, schedule some time on a regular basis to enjoy your favourite sport or leisure activity. All these things can help to restore perspective to the daily struggle to survive. They can also be a source of inspiration, and a place to discover connections.

- *Be a bit more conscious of the food you eat, just as you were in retreat.* Let the meal take a few minutes longer, if it means that you can make the time to taste before you swallow. Encourage your senses to stay as alive as they were while you were on retreat. Notice the smell and feel and sounds of the world around you.

- *If you kept any notes of your time in retreat, reread them from time to time,* and consider keeping up this practice of writing a kind of inner diary or journal, or of expressing in drawings or symbols anything that seems to be coming up in your prayer and reflection. Don't worry if you feel you can't write or can't draw. These records are only for your own eyes. They can become another form of prayer, as new connections arise for you in the process, and the act of writing or drawing takes on a life of its own.

Turning your contemplation into action

For many people a retreat brings to mind particular issues and may leave them with a specific sense of challenge. Immediately after a retreat it is well worth spending an hour or two quietly reflecting on what you feel the most significant fruits of your retreat have been. Try to answer for yourself a question like:

During this retreat what has been the one most important thing
I have learned, or God has opened up in my life?

Now take that 'one most important thing' back into prayer. Perhaps
you already have a sense of what it means for you, and how you
can take it further. If so, now would be the time to work out what
you are going to do about it in practice.

- If a relationship has been coming up in your prayer, for example,
  what do you feel you are being asked to do next in that relationship?
- If new directions have crystallized in your life, how are you going
  to turn them into reality?
- If an area of need in the world around you has been dominant,
  what role do you feel you are being asked to play in addressing
  that need?
- If new insights have been gained, how are you going to take them
  further, refine them, and perhaps communicate them to others?
- If you have made any resolutions, how are you going to imple-
  ment them?

It might be a good idea to draw up a real action plan, noting quite
specific ways in which you are hoping to put the gifts of your
retreat into practice. But be realistic. Better, by far, to focus on just
one thing you are hoping to incorporate into your life, and to give
all your energy to making it happen, than to try to change a whole
range of acts and attitudes, and dissipate your energy too widely.

This part of the process of reflecting on your retreat might be
summed up in three simple questions:

- What have I brought away from this retreat?
- Who, or what, is it for?
- How am I going to turn it into lived reality?

The ongoing journey

Life beyond a retreat will never be quite the same as it was before –
even though it can often feel as though the time in retreat is just a
distant memory. To help you continue to live out the good effects

of your retreat, you might like to consider one or more of the following ideas:

- Seek out the companionship of a 'soul friend', or spiritual companion/director. (For more details, see **Soul Friendship** in Part IV.) To meet regularly with someone who will listen with loving acceptance as you share your ongoing journey is a gift that should not be underestimated. If you have made an individually given retreat, you will know the value of personal companionship in the journey of the heart. A 'soul friend' enables you to continue to benefit from this gift, in the years that follow your retreat.
- Consider joining a group of like-minded pilgrims in **faith sharing meetings**. Group companionship offers enormous spiritual support and a space for growth and discernment.
- If there is a **spirituality network** in your area, you might like to find out what it is doing and more about its ethos and aims, and perhaps become a part of the network yourself.
- Try exploring new approaches to prayer – perhaps something that was suggested during your retreat, or something you find in one of the books suggested for further reading.
- Keep your own spirituality 'earthed', by checking out regularly to what extent it interacts with the needs of the society you live in, those in your area who are in any kind of need, or the needs of the created world. If your contemplation is not finding some expression in action that goes beyond your personal world, it is not being fully true to the gospel that inspires it.
- Consider how you are going to seek out time in retreat in future, possibly making it a regular part of your life's journey.

The work of the Retreat Association

The Retreat Association exists to provide resources and information for all those interested in the possibility of making a retreat. It also co-ordinates new initiatives and maintains networks. Its work includes, for example:

- Responding to requests to put individuals in touch with someone in their local area who can help them on their journey. The

Association maintains a network of regional contacts who are familiar with the different spiritual guides in their area and can offer advice based on this personal knowledge.

- Providing information on training opportunities for those who would like to explore the possibility of learning the skills of prayer guiding and spiritual companionship themselves.
- Publishing the annual edition of the *Retreats* magazine, and a range of leaflets on different aspects of the retreat movement.
- Offering advice by phone, fax or email, and maintaining a web site of relevant information.
- Organizing a conference every four years to draw together those who are involved in the work of the retreat movement.

The Association comprises the following member groups:

Association for Promoting Retreats (mainly Anglican)
Baptist Union Retreat Group
Methodist Retreat Group
National Retreat Movement (mainly Roman Catholic)
Quaker Retreat Group
United Reform Church Silence and Retreats Network

If you would like to support the network of the retreat movement and receive further information, the first step would be to join whichever of the member groups feels most appropriate. Each has its own network and organizes a range of events. Membership of any of the groups entitles you to receive a subscription to *Retreats*. Alternatively, *Retreats* can be purchased from most religious book stockists.

The contact addresses for the various member groups, and for the Retreat Association itself, are listed at the end of this book.

PART IV
Fact File

This part of the book is set out in the form of a fact file, with entries on a range of subjects, arranged in alphabetical order. These entries are cross-referenced from other sections of the book by the use of a bold typeface. Entries describing a particular type of retreat include an outline of what to expect in such a retreat, a guide to duration and cost, and an indication of where to look for more specific information. Other entries explain some of the terms commonly used in the world of retreat-making.

Christian Life Community

Christian Life Community (CLC) is the name of an organization inspired by the spirituality of St Ignatius Loyola, which fosters the growth of small groups of people who are trying to embody the value of the gospel in their own lives, using Ignatian principles to help them.

Each local CLC group meets together regularly to share their journeying and to help each other know Christ better and discover what he is asking of them in their daily lives.

CLC may be a way forward for you especially if:

- You are searching for something more from your faith;
- You want to deepen your faith and express it in your daily living;
- You are looking for more effective ways of bringing together your whole human life with the fullness of your Christian faith.

CLC groups include both men and women, married and single, of various ages and Christian denominations, but each with a desire to deepen their life of prayer and Christian discipleship. The group members offer each other companionship along the way, and are also aware of belonging to a regional, national and international CLC community, with opportunities to meet and share experience on a wider level and to make retreats with other CLC members.

Each local CLC is autonomous, and works out for itself what form of meeting bests suits its members. However, for those who wish, excellent material is available suggesting a focus for personal prayer between meetings, aids for prayer, questions to encourage reflection, and guidelines on how to get the best out of the meeting. A national chaplain, development workers and facilitators are available to assist on request, but will not impose themselves. Regional days of reflection are offered on a regular basis, and members receive a monthly newsletter called *Focus*.

Local groups meet in members' own homes, typically once a fortnight, and the pattern of the meeting will include some shared prayer, sharing on scripture, sharing on prayer experience since the last meeting, sharing joys and giving support in each other's difficulties (but not trying to 'fix' each other!). The principles underlying these meetings are as described under **Faith sharing meetings**.

Daily routine on retreat

Many people about to go on retreat find themselves wondering what a typical day will be like. While every retreat house has its own routine, and no two retreats are the same, it may be helpful to give a couple of *examples* of how a day might run on retreat. Please bear in mind that:

- These *are* only examples; and
- Especially in an individually given retreat, no fixed routine will be imposed on you. You are a free citizen and may choose to miss meals, to go off for an outing, or to do whatever you wish with your time.

A typical day on an individually given retreat

Between 7.30 and 9.00 a.m.	Breakfast
9.00 a.m. to 12.00 noon	Your own time
12.00 to 12.45	Daily Eucharist
13.00 to 14.00	Lunch
14.00 to 16.00	Your own time
16.00 to 16.30	Afternoon tea
16.30 to 19.00	Your own time
19.00 to 19.45	Supper
20.00 to 20.30	Shared evening prayer

Your meeting with your guide will be arranged during one of the periods of 'free time'.

As you can see, there is considerable time that is 'yours' to do as you wish. Some of this time will certainly be spent in prayer and reflection, but it is also wise to allow some time for rest and relaxation, and perhaps for taking a walk.

A typical day on a theme retreat

Between 7.30 and 9.00 a.m.	Breakfast
Until 10.00 a.m.	Free time
10.00 to 11.00	Presentation by the retreat guide
11.00 to 12.00 noon	Time for individual prayer and reflection
12.00 to 12.45	Daily Eucharist
13.00 to 14.00	Lunch
14.00 to 16.00	Free time
16.00 to 16.30	Afternoon tea
16.45 to 17.30	Presentation by the retreat guide
17.30 to 19.00	Group sharing or open forum
19.00 to 19.45	Supper
20.00 to 20.30	Shared evening prayer

As this sample timetable shows, there is rather less 'free time' on a theme retreat. This plan is also very flexible. Sometimes the retreat leader will give only one presentation, sometimes two or even three. There may well be an evening presentation, leaving the entire afternoon free.

In some cases the time between presentations will be in strict silence, sometimes not.

It should be stressed that everything is optional on retreat, within the constraints of common courtesy, and with proper regard for other people's need of rest and quiet. If you intend to miss a meal, for example, it would be appropriate to say so in advance, to avoid unnecessary waste of food. There is no obligation to attend the daily services or prayers, though the fact of gathering together in prayer is usually found to be a source of great strength and solidarity among retreatants.

If you are an 'owl', rather than an early bird, you may be surprised to discover how quiet a retreat house becomes after 10 p.m. (sometimes even earlier). The night silence must be observed, for the sake of all other guests and residents, but there will usually be a little 'brew bar' where you can make yourself tea or coffee at any time of the day or night, provided you do it quietly.

Enneagram retreats

The Enneagram is an oral tradition, probably developed in the East as many as 1,500 years ago, and brought into the western tradition early in the twentieth century. Used in the eastern tradition by mystics down the centuries, it is now becoming increasingly popular in the West. It offers a well-tried method of understanding more clearly the ways in which our personality and our early life experience influences the way we make our choices and relationships. It also, very valuably, gives insight into the most fruitful ways in which each personality type can potentially move forward into growth, and the likely ways in which each personality type will most readily regress under stress.

The tradition represents nine basic personality types in the form of a circle, in which each type also connects to two other types, that might be termed the 'growth path' and the 'regression path' respectively. The whole circle also divides into three segments representing three main 'centres' (the 'heart' or feeling centre, the 'head', or thinking centre and the 'gut' or instinctive centre).

An Enneagram retreat (which may be given non-residentially, over a period of time, or residentially over a weekend or longer) is an opportunity to explore the insights of the Enneagram and discover its truths within your own personality. It must be stressed that the Enneagram is an *oral tradition*. It is not something that can be gleaned from a book, but must be given by a trained practitioner, who will explain the tradition and look in turn at each of the nine personality types and their tendencies. It is not, however, a 'pigeon-holing' exercise. The subtleties of Enneagram wisdom go deep and can be very helpful indeed in gaining an awareness of why we react as we do, given particular personality traits and early conditioning.

Sometimes the giving of the Enneagram is combined with a longer **individually given retreat** to enable the retreatant to reflect more fully in prayer, with the **retreat guide**, on the ways in which the newly discovered insights are being worked out in the real events and relationships of the retreatant's life.

Because of the need for an expert administrator, the cost of an Enneagram retreat may be slightly higher than that of a more generalized retreat. Details of available Enneagram retreats are given in *Retreats*.

Faith sharing meetings

For many Christians the support of a small local group of fellow pilgrims is an essential part of their spiritual journey. There are a number of ways in which such groups can function. Prayer groups exist in many churches. House groups are becoming increasingly popular as a way of exploring faith questions more deeply. Bible study and discussion groups flourish in many Christian churches and other establishments.

So what is different about a 'faith sharing group', and what might you expect to find if you join one?

- The focus of a faith sharing group is always upon the sharing of the members' lived experience of God's action and movement in their lives and their hearts. To allow this experience to be shared in a non-threatening way, certain principles apply:
- The total confidentiality of everything that is shared must be assured. This principle, which is non-negotiable, needs to be clearly understood and endorsed by every member from the start.
- The group meeting offers 'safe space' in which each person can share as much or as little of their experience as they wish. To this end, most of the meeting is spent in giving time to each member to open up anything at all they wish to share. While a person is sharing, the others engage in 'active listening', seeking to give the sharer their whole attention. Active listening means listening without any trace of judgement, simply receiving what is being said in a spirit of loving acceptance.
- When an individual has said what he or she wishes to say, a brief period of silence is held, to hold what has been said in reverence and prayer. There is no discussion, and no attempt to 'put the

person right' or to offer solutions to problems. There is no argument or questioning, and the person sharing must never be interrupted.

- When all have shared what they wish to share, the meeting may open up into a more general sharing, if desired, but still with no discussion or attempts at therapy. The reason for the ban on discussion is that the ethos of such gatherings is to operate from the heart and not from the head. Discussions engaging reason and logic have an important place in our journeying as, for example, in Bible study groups, but the faith sharing group is a place where 'heart speaks to heart'.

- The meeting may end with shared prayer, silent or vocal, and a chance to relax over a cup of tea or coffee. Meetings normally take place in members' own homes, ideally with a rotation of host(ess) and facilitator.

Why are faith sharing groups so helpful, if nothing is discussed and no solutions are offered? Perhaps the heart of the matter is that this kind of sharing provides a space where we can reveal ourselves, as we are, at least to a certain extent, to trusted fellow pilgrims, and still continue to be unconditionally loved by them, even if, at the 'head' level, they might disagree with our thoughts. In such a group, the ideal is to offer each other something of God's unconditional love and acceptance, and to enable each other to grow more fully into who we really are. As soon as we offer to 'fix' each other, we are virtually saying (in the language of transactional analysis) 'You're not OK!' This runs completely against the spirit of faith sharing, which is based on the premise of 'I'm OK – You're OK'.

People who share their faith journey in groups like this often describe the experience as that of 'walking on holy ground'. When we are permitted to walk upon another person's holy ground of innermost experience, we 'take off our shoes', step sensitively, and say nothing. Our silence honours the gift they are giving us, which is nothing less than a glimpse of the core of their being, where God is indwelling.

First time retreats

Many retreat centres now offer retreats specially tailored for those who have never made a retreat before. While a 'standard' residential retreat tends to last for six or eight days, a 'first time retreat' will usually be shorter than this – perhaps just three or four days, or maybe just a weekend. The idea is to offer retreatants a taste of the experience of an **individually given retreat** in a silent, or near-silent situation, with the focus on prayer and reflection. The first time of making a retreat can be something of a 'culture shock', especially if you are used to a noisy and demanding environment or workplace. There may be a fear of 'How will I pray for that long?' or 'How will I fill the time?' or 'How will I handle the quietness?'

Those who offer first time retreats understand these anxieties very well, and such a retreat will often offer help in dealing with these matters. For example, your guide may suggest ways of structuring the day so as to reach a good balance of rest, prayer and recreation. Most first time retreats will also suggest approaches to personal prayer that you may not have tried before.

Often a first time retreat will include rather more time to be together with the others who are making the retreat, than would normally be the case. The silence will usually be broken up by periods of meeting together to reflect on various aspects of the process of making the retreat. There may be opportunities for sharing your feelings with the rest of the group, though there should never be any pressure to do so.

The *Retreats* magazine specifically indicates 'first time retreats' in its listings. If this is what you are looking for, try browsing the lists, until you find something that attracts you. You might then want to contact the retreat centre concerned to ask for more details. Don't hesitate to ask specific questions about how the retreat is run, to make sure that it is what you are hoping for, before you commit yourself.

In daily life a 'first time retreat' takes the same form as a normal **retreat in daily life**, except that your **prayer companion/prayer guide** will be especially aware that you are making this experience for the first time and will offer you extra guidance, if you want it, on how to get the best out of your retreat. You will find that many people making a retreat in daily life are doing so for the first time, because this approach to retreat-making is growing very fast.

Individually given retreats

The words 'individually given', or 'individually guided' might well strike fear into the heart of a would-be retreat-maker. Even more so, perhaps, if you hear these terms reduced to their initials, and are left wondering what on earth you are letting yourself in for if you enter upon an 'IGR'.

Simply, an individually given retreat is a period of retreat usually (though not necessarily) conducted in silence, in which you will have an individual companion who will be alongside you in prayer in a special way through the days of your retreat, and will be available for regular personal, one-to-one meetings with you. In a residential retreat, these meetings will usually be every day, though sometimes less frequently. In a daily life retreat, they will be daily in a week-long retreat, or perhaps weekly in a retreat lasting several weeks.

The first thing to say is that this companion will be a person of prayer, and of empathy, and will be looking forward to making the retreat journey with you, knowing what a genuine privilege it is to be invited to share in another person's sacred story. If you are wondering what kind of person this companion will be, and what his or her role is in the retreat, have a browse through the entries headed '**Retreat guide/retreat director**' and '**Prayer companion/prayer guide**'.

Before ever you arrive on your retreat, your companion will have been praying for you, and preparing for your arrival. You will be told, at the beginning of the retreat, who your companion will be, and you will meet personally very soon after your arrival. Probably your companion will suggest some ways of settling into the retreat, of relaxing, and of simply enjoying the experience, and possibly give you some scriptural, or other material as a focus for some gentle prayer during the first day of your retreat. A time will be arranged, when the two of you will meet. This will normally be at the same time every day in a residential retreat, or the same time every week in a daily life retreat.

During an individually given retreat, the meeting between retreatant and retreat guide is an important landmark in the routine of the day (week). Most people rapidly begin to look forward to these meetings, as an opportunity to gather the fruits of the previous day's (week's) prayer and focus on the best direction ahead. This is the opportunity to discern, together, what God seems to be doing in your prayer, what seems to be important for you, what challenges and choices are beginning to crystallize. The discernment process is yours alone, but your companion can help by replaying to you what seems to be at the heart of your sharing. It is you who are singing your heart's song, but your companion will be able to re-echo to you the dominant chords of that song. If you are feeling anxious about what you will say in these conversations, you might like to read the entry in Part II headed 'What will I talk about with my guide?'

Sometimes there may be no great need to talk, and the meeting can be kept quite brief. At other times, you may need more time and space to open up important issues with your guide. Remember that there is no pressure at all in these conversations. They are simply a space, and an accepting, non-judgemental listener, with whom you can explore anything you feel you want to explore. Your retreat is not an achievement course and there are no 'expectations'. This type of retreat is 'individual', in that it incorporates one-to-one sharing, but it is also 'given'. What is 'given' is not a course, or a programme of direction, or a schedule of prayer, but space, time and whole-hearted attention, together with gentle suggestions, if appropriate, as to how to move on in your next day's journey with God.

Your companion will also be seeing a supervisor on a regular basis. The purpose of **supervision** is *solely* to give the guide space to explore his/her own feelings and reactions arising from the process of accompanying others. It is in no way concerned with the matters raised between the guide and the retreatant, and everything you share with your companion will remain strictly between the two of you.

You may be invited, at the end of your retreat, to comment on how you have found the process, using some kind of evaluation sheet. Please take advantage of this opportunity if you can. It is very helpful to the retreat guides and to those organizing the retreat to have feedback on how the retreatants have experienced it.

Julian Meetings/silent prayer groups

Ever since Jesus himself spent periods of solitude in lonely places, and some of the early Christian hermits followed his example, contemplative prayer has been part of the Christian heritage. Until recently, however, this has largely been practised only in monastic communities.

In the later part of the twentieth century there was a strong upsurge of interest in eastern forms of mysticism, which made western Christians begin to realize that the practice of contemplation had been seriously neglected in the western tradition. In 1973 a movement began to redress this balance, and people in 11 areas of the UK set up contemplative prayer groups. These were the first Julian groups, and today, 30 years later, there are over 4,000 Julian Meetings in the UK, and a growing number worldwide.

Julian Meetings take their name from Julian of Norwich, a fourteenth-century mystic. Dame Julian is a model of contemplative prayer, and her writings are sometimes used in the meetings, but Julian Meetings are far from being a cult of Dame Julian.

The purpose of the meetings is to 'foster the practice and teaching of contemplative prayer within the Christian tradition'. This reflects the assertion of Dame Julian that the highest form of prayer consists in simply waiting on God.

People who attend Julian Meetings are usually active members of their own churches, though some have no formal links with organized Christianity. The movement arranges local and regional quiet days or retreats, and an annual national retreat, at which people from different meetings have an opportunity to meet and share their experience.

A small group of volunteers makes sure that enquiries are responded to, and the regular JM magazine (published three times a year) and other literature are sent out. Julian Meetings employ no paid staff and have no offices.

A Julian Meeting is a time of silent prayer, and people find that this can greatly help them learn to be still with God. The isolation that so often besets a contemplative life is eased by the fellowship of the meeting, and the prayerful silence is helped and amplified when two or three come together. A meeting can be a place to share any problems you are experiencing in prayer, and to benefit from the encouragement of others.

The meetings themselves take place either in a private home or in a church or chapel. They may include a brief reading, a piece of music, and certainly about half an hour of silent prayer. Afterwards there may be an opportunity for tea, coffee and conversation. Each meeting is free to arrange things in its own way. No specific method of meditation is taught. People are encouraged to find what is right for them, and how they can integrate contemplative prayer into their daily living.

A nominal charge is made to subscribe to the JM magazine and obtain a list of UK Julian Meetings. Details of your nearest Julian Meeting will be supplied free on request.

Other organizations offering opportunities to join silent prayer groups include:

Christian Meditation
Fellowship of Contemplative Prayer
Hear Our Silence (focusing on Carthusian prayer)
Servants of Christ the King

For more details of any of the above contact the Retreat Association and ask for the leaflet *Silent Prayer Groups*.

Myers Briggs Typology Indicator ®
(MBTI ™)

The Myers Briggs personality type indicator (abbreviated to MBTI) offers a way of gaining insight into the way we make decisions and relationships by looking at our preferred ways of doing things. These apparently inbuilt preferences that people display are categorized according to four orientations that derive from the psychology of Carl Gustav Jung, and are based on:

- The fundamental division between *extrovert* and *introvert* personality types
- The two basic human processes of *perceiving* and *judging*
- The two poles of the perceiving process: *sensing* and *intuition*
- The two poles of the judging process: *thinking* and *feeling*

Depending on the personal tendency to prefer one of these over the other in a given category, a four-letter personality type indicator is derived. The way in which this indicator is determined is by means of a series of questions, administered and evaluated by a trained Myers Briggs practitioner.

A Myers Briggs retreat is an opportunity to enter into this process, first by listening to an explanation of the process itself, then by answering the questions, and finally by reflecting on how these insights are affecting the way we live.

Like the **Enneagram**, the Myers Briggs process is not intended to put people into boxes or make generalized statements about how particular personality types will behave. It is a way of deepening our own insight into how we tend to react, and why and, perhaps even more importantly, to deepen our understanding of others, recognizing the unique giftedness of each. An interesting development of the Myers Briggs process can lead on to the discovery of how our spiritual lives can be calling us into an increasing use of the non-preferred sides of our personality, as we move further towards the ideal of psychological and spiritual integration.

Because of the need for an expert administrator, the cost of a Myers Briggs retreat may be slightly higher than that of a more generalized retreat. Details of available Myers Briggs retreats are given in *Retreats*.

Open door retreats

An open door retreat involves:

- Attendance at a two-hour session once a week for nine consecutive weeks, during which you will meet with others who are also making the retreat. You will be asked to undertake to attend all sessions and to arrive punctually, unless unforeseen circumstances arise.

- A commitment to spend at least 15 minutes each day in personal prayer and reflection.
- A willingness to share something of the experience of the week's prayer with the group.
- An agreement to be bound to absolute confidentiality with regard to everything that is shared in the group meetings.

The weekly meetings are led usually by a team of two people who have made an open door retreat themselves and have also been trained in the leading of this kind of retreat. The leaders will also be making the retreat with you, and will share something of their own experience of prayer and of the challenge to live a Christ-centred life.

The leaders will be available, if needed, to help individuals on a one-to-one basis, as well as facilitating the meetings, listening sensitively to all that is shared and encouraging all the group along its journey.

The retreat takes the general form of an opening session, which mainly offers an introduction to the process, and will give you an idea of what to expect. During the week following this first meeting you will probably want to reflect on whether this is a journey you feel you want to make. If you feel that you are not able to enter into this kind of commitment at this time, or if you have doubts of any other nature, you are completely free to opt out at this point. The whole purpose of the first session is to give you time to reflect, and to feel free not to continue.

If you decide to go on, the next seven weeks will open up a particular aspect of the journey with God: for example, God's creative love, God's forgiving love, God's inviting and challenging love, and so on. You will be offered a set of handouts suggesting focus points for the following week's prayer. These may include scripture passages and other inspirational material, and guidance on different approaches to prayer. The final meeting will be a chance to review the experience and reflect on the gifts received and shared.

A small charge is made for an open door retreat, simply to cover any expenses involved in supplying the handouts and covering the travel expenses of the team. In case of need help can sometimes be offered.

The Retreat Association will be able to give you a contact address for more information.

Prayer companion/prayer guide

You may come across the term 'prayer companion/prayer guide' as an alternative name for retreat guide or companion in a retreat house setting or, more commonly, if you are making a **retreat in daily life**, or a 'week of guided prayer'. The prayer companion is your companion along the way, and much of what is said under the heading **'Retreat guide/retreat director'** applies equally to prayer companions. And, like the term 'spiritual director', the term 'guide' is a misnomer, because whatever else the prayer companion does, he or she will never attempt to 'guide' or 'direct' your prayer.

A 'prayer companion' tends to be a person – often a lay person – who has had some training in listening skills and in attending whole-heartedly, with empathy and without judgement, to another person's journey in faith. Most prayer companions are in normal employment or are running homes and raising families, or are retired people. They offer their time as retreat guides in addition to their daily life commitments, often on a voluntary basis. They will not usually have done any 'professional' training in spirituality, counselling or psychology. They are there simply as listening companions, often people who are grappling with the same kind of problems in life as you are yourself.

The term 'prayer companion/prayer guide' is sometimes used to distinguish between the companion who accompanies retreatants only for the duration of a week (or weeks) or guided prayer, from a person who engages in ongoing spiritual companionship of others over a longer period (see also **Soul friendship**).

Training in prayer accompanying is offered in several centres in the UK and entails, usually, a course of evening meetings over eight or more weeks, during which the principles of active listening are introduced and practised intensively, and the main aspects of the spiritual journey are explored. Trainees will usually also be asked to attend at least one residential weekend during which they will make the experience of giving someone else a short retreat, and allowing another student to given them a retreat. Ideally, those showing a gift for this kind of companionship, will then be asked to help as a trainee member of a team of prayer companions offering a 'live' daily life retreat in the neighbourhood. Follow-up training is often offered leading, in some cases, to more far-reaching courses and practical training under supervision.

Quiet days

A quiet day can take any form, but it will always offer you a space of reflective calm, and usually also some kind of input to help you find inner stillness and to deepen your spiritual life in some way.

Quiet days fall into several categories:

- Days centred on a particular theme, often with a short talk or talks given by a speaker or retreat leader. A 'theme day' like this may begin with a short time of quiet, to help participants settle in. A talk or presentation may follow, with time afterwards for private reflection and/or group sharing or an open forum where questions and comments can be raised.
- Days offering simply a quiet place, with no input, or at most a period of led prayer. There may also be an opportunity to speak with someone one-to-one if you wish.
- Days centred on a particular activity. A day of this nature would include possibly some kind of instruction or guidance in the activity concerned, and its spiritual dimension. It would also include plenty of opportunity to meet with others who also enjoy the same activity.
- So-called 'taster days' to allow you to try out new approaches to prayer, for example. These are an excellent introduction to personal prayer, and may be a good place to begin your explorations if you are thinking of making a retreat for the first time.

The best way to find a quiet day to suit your needs is to browse through the *Retreats* magazine and see what is on offer. The range of possibilities will probably leave you feeling spoiled for choice.

A 'quiet day', typically, lasts from about 10 a.m. to 4 p.m. The cost can vary enormously, from as little as £4 up to £20 or more. This will depend very much on what is being included (some quiet days include morning coffee, lunch and afternoon tea) and on the cost of hiring the location and covering the expenses of any speakers. If lunch is not included, you would be expected to take your own packed lunch, or possibly to take a contribution of food towards a 'bring and share' lunch.

Many centres that are used for quiet days are very welcoming of people who wish merely to 'drop in to quietness' perhaps just for a short while, and then go on their way.

There is a National Quiet Day, held each year on the third Saturday in June. This is an opportunity for people who may not otherwise have thought of doing so, to try the experience of meditative quietness for themselves. Look out for local details of special events around this date.

Quiet gardens

A particular kind of ministry of hospitality has opened up in recent years through the work of the Quiet Garden Trust. This Trust came into being in 1992, to help provide support and encouragement to those willing to open up their homes and gardens, large or small, to welcome people seeking silence, solitude, space for reflection, or an informal time of quiet together with others of like mind. The idea, which was pioneered by the Revd Philip Roderick, has now spread to many other countries, and hospitality is being offered by the owners of homes and gardens in Australia, Botswana, Brazil, Canada, Haiti, India, Ireland, Israel, Kenya, New Zealand, South Africa, Uganda, the USA and Zambia, as well as all over the British Isles. A number of retreat houses are affiliated to the Quiet Garden Movement. For details, see also *Retreats*.

Homes and gardens offering hospitality open their gates on certain days, some as often as twice a week, others perhaps once a month, so that people may make a quiet retreat there, sometimes guided and focused by a facilitator, sometimes simply offering space to be still. Each location decides for itself how it wishes to structure the hospitality offered. Very often those who benefit from such a day feel moved to offer their own gardens for the same purpose, and so the movement spreads.

Philip Roderick describes something of the range of these places of quiet hospitality:

> Britain's quiet gardens can be found in a whole variety of venues, from a small house and garden in the suburbs to an 80 acre farm; from a house on the coast near Deal with a pebbled beach for its front garden, to a converted barn in Yorkshire. All may be contexts of prayer and nurture. Around the hearth or in the sunlight, concerns are shared, stories are told and prayer support offered.

All are welcome in a quiet garden. As with most retreat opportunities, this ministry transcends denominational divisions. Today, when many churches are locked during the week, and the few retreat houses are fully booked, or too far away, or financially out of reach, the quiet garden offers an excellent alternative way of finding time in stillness with God.

Retreat guide/retreat director

So you have decided to make a retreat, either residentially or in daily life, and you have opted for an **individually given retreat**. What about your guide-to-be? Who is this person who is going to be alongside you during this period of more intensive prayer? What will he or she be like?

Before any retreat there is always – even in the most experienced of retreat-makers – a sense of some mild apprehension as to who the guide will be and how the relationship will work out. You could be forgiven for imagining that this 'guide' or 'director' is some kind of wonder-being who knows all the answers, and never

sets a foot wrong in their own prayer or their Christian living. And
you couldn't be more wrong!

Let us begin, if we may, by demolishing the word 'spiritual director'. No one is going to 'direct' you. And the journey you are
making is not something exclusively 'spiritual'. It concerns the
whole of you. And the 'guide' is there simply to be alongside you,
to listen to whatever you may want to share, to accept and affirm
you unconditionally (though not to flatter you either!). This is
quite definitely a peer relationship, and in no way a relationship of
any kind of authority. It bears repeating that there is only ever one
Guide and one Director in the encounter with God and that is
God's own Holy Spirit. The retreat guide is there to be with you,
helping you to discern the movements of the Holy Spirit in your
own life, by simply reflecting back to you what seems to be
happening.

You will discover who your guide is to be during the first meeting
of the retreat. This will happen either at the opening meeting of a
daily life retreat, or on the first evening of a residential retreat. You
will not normally have a choice of guide, though if you have real
reason to feel that the appointed guide is the wrong person for
you, you are free, of course, to say so and to ask the organizer
whether it might be possible to change. This might be the case, for
example, if you find you know the guide personally in some other
context. Please bear in mind that once a retreat has begun it is very
difficult to rearrange the guides and retreatants.

It may help you to feel more at ease with your guide if you are
aware of a few facts beforehand about 'guides' in general:

- *Retreat guides are also retreatants themselves.* They make their own retreats, usually on a regular basis, and they share their own spiritual
  journeys with a 'soul friend' or 'spiritual director'. They also
  have a 'supervisor' (see **Supervision**). As people who regularly
  make retreats and share their own prayer life, they know how it
  feels to find yourself nervously waiting for a retreat to begin.
- *Most retreat guides find themselves in this role 'by accident'.* People don't
  wake up one morning and decide that they will become retreat
  guides. Usually they are people who have found great challenge
  and joy in their own journeying with God and feel a desire to
  help others grow in their Christian life. When this happens they

may intensify their own searching, possibly by attending courses to help them listen more attentively, both to God's voice within themselves, and to the ways in which God is active in others. Usually they will find that people are seeking them out, often informally, to share something of the spiritual quest. Then, when a retreat is planned, the organizers look around for people like this who might be willing to help on the team of 'companions' or 'listeners'. So, often to their own surprise, they find themselves cast in the role of 'retreat guide'.

- *All retreat guides should have had some training*, to help them develop their listening skills. (If you wish to reassure yourself on this point, feel free to phone the retreat house concerned and ask.) Several things are emphasized during this training. The first, and most important, is the requirement for absolute confidentiality. You can be assured that nothing you share with your guide will ever go any further. Other aspects of the training include the nurturing of empathy, which means that *your* guide will 'walk a mile in your moccasins' trying always to enter into your experience from your point of view. You will be unconditionally accepted and welcomed without any form of judgement. You can say whatever you want, express whatever views and feelings you need to, without fear of offending your guide.

  A final aspect of the training will have enabled your guide to pick up those moments in what you are saying (or, indeed, in what you are not saying) that seem to indicate deep feeling or strong reaction, or some other sign of inner movement, and to reflect back to you what you were saying when that moment happened. This can be extraordinarily helpful in opening up for you an area that can now be safely explored. Often we don't know what we want to say until we hear ourselves say it. The guide is there to help you hear yourself say it.

- *The guide is fallible*, and may be struggling too with the big, and the little, questions of faith. The most effective guides are often the ones who are most wounded themselves. Guides are not people who have 'got it all together', but those who know how it feels to fall apart, and surrender to God's remaking. It will not be helpful for either of you if you, even unconsciously, put the guide on a pedestal. This will distract you from the purpose of your retreat, which is to come closer to God, not to the guide. Regard him or her as a friend who is also on the journey, also stumbling over the stones and stopping to admire the views.

- *Nevertheless, your guide, however flawed, will be a person of prayer*, who takes *your* prayer and *your* journey deeply seriously. For many people it is a quite new experience in retreat, to be able to share things about their journey with God, and have a listener alongside who is receiving 'on the same wavelength'.
- *Finally, retreat guides may be male or female, lay or ordained, of any age* (though most commonly people in the second half of life are engaged in this ministry) of any denomination and from any cultural or ethnic background. What they are *not*, is a race apart!

Retreats in daily life

Retreats in daily life offer a means of making a definite period of retreat, in which to deepen prayer and spiritual life, without having to go away to a residential setting or leave one's normal day-to-day commitments. This kind of retreat is also often called a Week (or Weeks) of Guided Prayer.

A retreat in daily life is a variation of the **individually given retreat**, in that you will have a personal companion to accompany you through the period of the retreat. The most commonly used models for this kind of retreat are:

- The week of guided prayer, which lasts for five, six or seven consecutive days, and entails a daily meeting with your companion or **prayer companion/prayer guide**.
- The extended retreat in daily life, which is spread over four, five or six weeks, or even longer, and entails, usually, a weekly meeting with your companion.

Both of these ways of offering a daily life retreat begin with a welcome meeting for all those making the retreat, and for their companions or 'prayer companions'. Usually this meeting will include some time for reflection, an explanation of how the retreat will proceed, and an opportunity to meet your companion and arrange the times you will meet during the retreat. A similar gathering will happen at the end of the retreat, when the whole group will come together again, to share in reflection, to talk about the experience if they wish to do so, and perhaps to have a small celebration together.

All that is asked of you, in making a daily life retreat is:

- To commit yourself to a time of prayer each day during the retreat. Some guides may suggest a minimum period of about 10 to 15 minutes, and they will be glad to help you find fruitful approaches to prayer, and to reflective living.
- To commit yourself to meet your guide promptly at the arranged time, and to share with him or her anything that you feel comfortable in sharing.

The venue for a daily life retreat might be almost anywhere. The most common venue is in a church hall, a vicarage, presbytery or manse, or a school hall or parish hall of some kind, at least for the opening and closing meetings. The one-to-one meetings with your guide may be arranged in a private home – either your own or the guide's, or any other mutually convenient location.

In general, the organization and the companioning ministry in a daily life retreat is offered on a voluntary basis. This means that the cost to you should be low, amounting only to a sum sufficient to cover the necessary expenses of the people involved, and the hiring of the venue. If you are concerned about cost, do ask the organizers, however, as some people, who usually have no other means of support, do make a charge or ask for a donation when offering spiritual companionship.

The idea of a daily life retreat is gaining ground, and you may find that one of your local churches is offering this possibility. If not, and if you know of a **spirituality network** or a 'Churches Together' organization in your area, contact its organizers and ask for details of any daily life retreats that may be coming up. If there are none, ask for one, and you will probably find that the network will be glad to initiate plans to get a retreat going.

Where two or more are gathered with the desire to make a retreat, then a retreat can happen. There is no need to wait until there is a queue of would-be retreatants. Be persistent if necessary, and don't take 'No' for an answer. Think ecumenically, and if your own tradition and its local leaders seem to be unwilling, or unable, to offer daily life retreats, approach the others. There is nothing in the rules of any tradition that forbids us to pray together!

Soul friendship

The ancient ministry of soul friendship is about ongoing spiritual companionship along the way. In the Celtic tradition, the soul-friend, or *anam cara*, was felt to be essential if one was serious about the journey of the soul. A Celtic saying tells us that 'a person without a soul friend is like a body without a head'. Today that ministry is growing and flourishing again, and is also known variously as 'spiritual direction', 'mentoring' or 'spiritual companionship'.

What makes a soul friend? Well, it is probably true to say that soul friends are both born and made. Anyone whom others will seek out as a companion along the way will usually have certain gifts. These gifts include, for example:

- The ability and the desire to give undivided, loving attention to the person who is sharing the journey.
- The ability to hold all that is shared in total confidence.
- The gift of empathy, allowing the soul friend to walk awhile in the pilgrim's shoes. Empathy is not the same as sympathy. Empathy means that the listener steps, inwardly, into the place of the speaker, and is thus able to see things from the speaker's point of view.
- The gift of 'unconditional positive regard', enabling the listener to be present and accepting of the speaker even if the speaker is expressing opinions or feelings that are radically different from the listener's own.
- The ability to be oneself, with no need to put on masks or hide behind false images. The natural soul friend will be at ease with herself, with no discrepancy between how she projects herself and how she really is. He will be willing to face, with God, and with his own soul friend, those parts of himself that he might prefer not to look at.
- The gift of prayerfulness. No one can accompany another on their journey of prayer unless they are prayerful themselves. A soul friend will usually be of a contemplative disposition, able to be quietly alongside another without interference.

This gifting can perhaps be summed up in the comment sometimes made about a good soul friend: 'When you are with her she makes you feel as though you are the only person in the world and she has all the time in the world to be alongside you.'

Soul friends may be either male or female, and are often lay people with no status in 'the church'. They usually find themselves drawn into this ministry simply because people seek them out and entrust to them the sacred space of their soul's journey.

Often, though not always, these gifts will have been encouraged and developed by some kind of training. The gifted soul friend, even untrained, will be sought after. The trained soul friend without the gifting will not.

How do you set about finding a soul friend? Perhaps the first thing to say is that you, the pilgrim, and no one else, choose your soul friend. Not the church, not the bishop, not the parish priest, but *you*. There may well be people around you who are known already as being willing and able to accompany others on their journey of faith, and it may be that you would seek out one such person and ask them whether they would be willing and able to accompany you. But often you will find yourself gravitating to 'the right person' almost intuitively. Look around your own circle of friends and acquaintances. Perhaps there is someone who, you feel, would be 'on your wavelength' spiritually, someone who is a person of prayer, someone who can listen gently and non-judgementally, without being tempted to offload his own agenda onto you. Often the right soul friend is found in an unexpected quarter.

If you feel you know who might be right for you, begin by asking them how they would feel about offering you this ministry. Remember that there is a limit to how many pilgrims a soul friend can reasonably accompany, so if the answer is 'No', don't take it personally. They may be able to suggest another person. If the answer is 'Yes', you will want to make arrangements about how often you will meet. This varies, of course, from person to person. People who are meeting a soul friend regularly may choose to meet every few weeks, every few months, or even just once a year. The length of these meetings again depends on what suits you both, but an hour would be a typical duration.

A common practice, at the beginning of an arrangement to meet with a soul friend is to suggest a 'trial period' of about three meetings together, while each of you reflects on how the relationship feels, and whether it will be fruitful to take it further.

Some people ask for some financial consideration for the time they give to this ministry. Others do not. This often depends on whether the person has any other means of support, and whether they themselves have to pay for their own spiritual direction and supervision. You need to establish expectations in this regard at the outset.

It is customary for the pilgrim to go to the soul friend's home or office for the session of 'spiritual direction', though a soul friend will often be willing to go to people who are housebound or without transport, to see them in their own home.

The relationship between pilgrim and soul friend is, for the most part, one-way. The pilgrim shares whatever she wishes with the soul friend, but the soul friend will not normally share much of his own journeying, unless this will help to set the pilgrim at ease, or add any genuine clarification to a particular issue. This is not a sign of distrust or secrecy on the part of the soul friend, but part of the process of practising empathy. He cannot walk in your shoes if he is preoccupied with his own!

If you are looking for a soul friend but can find no leads in your own area, the Retreat Association may be able to help you, by giving you a local contact name. This person will be aware of who is offering the ministry of companionship in your area, and will know such people personally.

Spiritual Exercises in daily life

The full **Spiritual Exercises of St Ignatius Loyola** can be made in daily life, without the need to go into the seclusion of a retreat house. For many people, the cost of five weeks' residence in a retreat house is prohibitive. Others may be quite unable to make such a long period of time free. Others, again, may be struggling against family indifference, or even hostility, to their spiritual searching, and couldn't even begin to think of taking so much time out of the family routine.

All these problems were around in Ignatius' own times (the sixteenth century). In particular, he was eager to make the experience of the Exercises possible for those in full-time occupations or, as he put it, those whose business responsibilities made it impossible for them to tuck themselves away in a boarding house (for that was all that was on offer to serve as a 'retreat house' in those times) for weeks on end. He added a note to the end of his text of the Exercises – the 'Nineteenth Annotation' (so called because it was the nineteenth of 20 such additional notes). The Nineteenth Annotation suggests that those who are unable to get away from the world for 30 or more days can be given the Exercises just as effectively in the context of their daily lives. Ignatius used this approach with a number of the people to whom he gave the Exercises himself.

Making the full Exercises in daily life is no less rigorous a process than making them in retreat, except that the journey of prayer and reflection involved lasts for at least six months, more typically for about nine months and sometimes even longer. Instead of making five periods of prayer each day, for about an hour each, the retreatant undertakes to make one period of prayer of about an hour each day, and to give some time to reflecting on what seemed to be happening in that period of prayer. Instead of a daily meeting with the retreat guide, there is a one-to-one meeting every week, or every two weeks. Otherwise the process is exactly as for a residential 30-day retreat.

If you are considering making this kind of extended **retreat in daily life**, you will first need to find someone who is willing to accompany you as a guide. This is a big commitment for both of you, and it may not be easy to find a guide. Remember, when seeking a guide for this particular journey, that the guide *must* have made the journey of the Exercises themselves, preferably individually with an experienced director, and must be thoroughly familiar with the dynamic of the Exercises. He or she should also be a person with whom you feel some rapport. You are going to be journeying together for a long time, and the relationship between you will go deep, as you share your innermost holy ground. It is worth waiting until the right person appears on the scene.

You would also do well to ask yourself why you actually want to make the Exercises. It would be a big mistake to view this journey as some kind of 'achievement', leading to the sense of some kind of 'spiritual qualification'. The end of the Exercises is always a new beginning, not a destination in itself. Your guide will be looking with you at your reasons, and helping you to discern, initially, whether this is the right thing to do, and the right time to do it.

Once you have embarked on the journey, you will need to find the time and space for in-depth prayer each day. This may well mean getting up an hour earlier than usual, or sacrificing an hour's TV time in the evening, to find the undisturbed time that you will need.

A few points may be worth bearing in mind:

- If you already have a **soul friend**, or 'spiritual director', talk to him/her about your desire to make the full Exercises. For the duration of the Exercises, it is probably advisable only to see your Exercises guide on a regular basis, and your normal companion will understand this. During the Exercises your prayer attention will be sharply focused on the meditations offered to you each week. Talking separately to two different people during this period may lead to confusion and distraction.

- In daily life no outside discipline will be imposed on you, as it would be in a retreat house. The self-discipline involved is also part of the journey. Many people discover that the commitment to prayer is bringing them such joy and such grace, that they are more than happy to give the time to it. However, almost everyone will go through periods of disillusionment and dryness at some stage in the process, and if this happens, talk it through with your guide, trying to trust that God who launched you into the prayer will also carry you forwards, until consolation returns.

- Before you think of making the full Exercises, make at least two or three shorter retreats in the Ignatian tradition, either in daily life or in residence. These will help you become familiar with the approaches to prayer and reflection that are helpful in making the Exercises, and will help you discover whether this kind of journey really is for you.

- If you make a shorter **individually given retreat** during the period of your Nineteenth Annotation journey, do tell the retreat guide that you are currently making the Exercises. The guide will probably try to ensure that anything suggested in your retreat is compatible with where you are in the Exercises, so that your overall direction is not disturbed.

The cost of making the Exercises in daily life is, of course, considerably less than a 30-day retreat in a retreat centre. Some people will ask for a donation or fee for their time, others will not. It is important to establish from the start what your guide expects. If you visit a guide in a retreat house for your weekly or fortnightly meetings, you should expect to make a financial contribution, since people in this situation are doing this kind of work for a living and often have no other means of support. Most retreat houses make it clear what their scale of expected donations is. If you are housebound, it may be possible to find a guide who is prepared to come to you in your own home.

Another way of making the Exercises in daily life is in a group setting. A group would not normally include more than six people, and one guide would lead them all through the scheme of the Exercises. They would share their prayer experience together every week or fortnight. For many people this is a very fruitful way of journeying. It should be borne in mind, however, that the original intention was that the Exercises should be given one-to-one, and this remains by far the best approach. If you have the chance to make the Exercises in a group, you might like to ask whether there will also be an opportunity to meet the group guide on a one-to-one basis fairly regularly, so that you can explore any issues that you might not feel happy about opening up in the full group.

Spiritual Exercises of St Ignatius Loyola

Why would anyone thinking of making a retreat in the twenty-first century be interested in a Basque who lived over 500 years ago? In fact, Ignatius, born Inigo Lopez, was largely responsible for a great deal that goes on in most **individually given retreats** today.

Inigo was born in 1491 in the Basque region of northern Spain, the youngest of a family of 13. As a young man he was trained in the arts of chivalry and seemed set for a glittering military career. Fate intervened, however, in the form of a cannon ball that shattered his leg while he was defending the fortress of Pamplona in a desperate bid to push back a French invasion. Inigo was grounded, and carried back unceremoniously across the hills to the family home in the castle of Loyola, where he was to spend many months in pain and boredom, convalescing from his injuries.

This sudden shattering of Inigo's dreams, however, was to become the beginning of a new dream – God's Dream in his life. He experienced a profound spiritual conversion, and decided to commit his life to God. Leaving behind his family and home in Loyola, and his hopes of worldly glory and conquest, he set off on a pilgrimage into the unknown – a pilgrimage that in due course brought him to a place called Manresa. Here, on the plain near Montserrat, he reflected deeply on his experience of brokenness, and of God's remaking, of how he had discovered the possibility of dreaming God's Dream, and the effects that was having on the inner movements in his heart and soul. During this period, living in a cave near the river, he embarked on a journey of prayer and re-flection and of learning to discern God's creative action in his own heart, and to distinguish it from the stirrings of the destructive movements he also observed within himself.

As Inigo prayed, and reflected – he also wrote down his own ex-perience, which eventually became the little book that we call 'The Spiritual Exercises'. It is no exaggeration to say that in Manresa Inigo was making an intensive, and extensive, retreat. And 'The Spiritual Exercises' were, in effect, his 'retreat notes'. He was learning the art of discernment, taught by God directly. He was discovering the agony and the ecstasy of connecting to God's movements in his life, and the possibility of making choices and decisions in accor-dance with what seemed to be God's action within him, while acting against any movements that appeared not to be coming from God.

In later years, Inigo was to gather a few companions around him, who were also eager to discover the mystery of God's action in their personal living, and God's direction in their life choices. Even-tually these companions joined together formally and took vows to work and journey together in their spiritual pilgrimage, encouraging others to do the same. They called themselves Companions of Jesus, and were the nucleus of what became the Society of Jesus, a religious order in the Roman Catholic Church, better known today as the Jesuits. In these early beginnings, Inigo himself led them through their own experience of what had been happening for him at Manresa. He shared his 'retreat notes' with them. He gave them his Exercises, not as a programme of education, but as a catalyst through which they might discover for themselves the power of God's Life becoming incarnate in their own living. And he encouraged them, in their turn, to give the Exercises to others.

The process of discernment that Inigo was learning in Manresa has thus become a model of discernment for the generations that followed after. The first Jesuits opened up the process for many of their generation, and today's Jesuits continue to do the same. Like their predecessors, they encourage those who benefit from making this particular experience to share it with others. In our generation there has been an amazing upsurge of interest in the treasures of what is now called 'Ignatian spirituality', and the process of discernment and decision, nurtured by scriptural meditation and one-to-one companionship, has become a model for many, if not most, of the individually given retreats that are offered today.

So what are the Exercises? The first thing to say is that if you come across 'the text' of the Exercises (and there are a number of contemporary versions on the market), don't even think about trying to read it 'raw'. In their printed form the Exercises comprise a set of structured scriptural meditations, interspersed with a few very powerful non-scriptural meditations, and some extensive guidance on how to discern the inner movements that are coming from God, and those that are not. If you try to 'read' the Exercises, even in their modern translations, you will almost certainly give up. The imagery and language is not readily accessible to the modern mind, and the Exercises are – and always were – an oral tradition, intended to be 'given', not read. This 'giving' of the Exercises is the essence of what happens in an individually *given* retreat, especially one given in the Ignatian tradition, as the majority are, directly or indirectly.

The so-called 'Full Exercises of St Ignatius' comprise a series of meditations and reflections that would normally take around 30 days to complete in a residential setting, with a **retreat guide/retreat director** as a personal companion throughout the process. The retreatant will make up to five periods of intensive prayer each day (around an hour each time) and will reflect on the fruits of that prayer, sharing them with the guide in a daily meeting. The meditations themselves invite the retreatant to reflect on the big questions of life, such as:

- What is the baseline of my existence? What is the purpose of my life?
- Where is my real security in life? Am I clinging to any 'false securities'?
- What may be blocking my relationship with God?
- What do I really desire, at the deepest level of my being? What does God desire for me?
- What movements and currents of my life are tending to lead me closer to God and to others? How can I nourish these movements and learn to 'go with them'?
- What movements and currents in my life are tending to drift me further away from God and from others? How can I learn to 'act against them'?
- How do I desire to respond to God's action in my life? What 'return' would I want to make for all that has been given to me?

These questions are explored by praying the scriptures in a personal and meditative way, seeking to make connections between what is happening, for example, in a particular Gospel passage, and what is happening in my own life right now. The process is also under-pinned by helping the retreatant to reflect regularly on where and how God's action has been evident in the day's journeying, so as to encourage the practice of ongoing discernment.

The full Exercises can be made either in a retreat centre, over a period of 30 days, or in daily life, in which case the process will nor-mally take between six and nine months, or possibly longer (see **Spiritual Exercises in daily life**).

To make the full Exercises in what is commonly called the '30-day Retreat' or the 'Long Retreat', you will actually need to be in the re-treat centre, for something like 35 or 36 days. This time will begin with a period of about three days for preliminary work, perhaps re-viewing your own faith story with your guide and possibly with others who will be making the retreat. It will end with a 'winding down period' to give you space to reflect on the total experience, and maybe share your reflections with the others in the group, if you are making the retreat in a group setting. The central 30 days will be conducted in complete silence, except for your daily meetings with the guide and your participation in the daily liturgy. There will, however, normally be three or four break days, often called 'repose days', when the silence will be lifted and you will be encouraged to relax. Repose days tend to mark the end of each phase of the Exercises. If you are trying to reach a major decision in your life, the Exercises will encourage you to focus on that decision and actively seek to discern God's guidance for it. Your guide will be alongside you in that discernment, helping you in the discernment, though in no way influencing its outcome.

Making the Exercises like this is a rigorous process, and quite an exhausting one. Ideally you will be given the freedom to proceed through the Exercises at your own pace, lingering longer with some and passing more quickly over others, depending on what is happening in your life and your prayer. Your guide will help you pace yourself appropriately. From the beginning, Ignatius envisaged that some people would benefit from making the full Exercises from start to end, while others would benefit most from remaining with one part or phase of the process. His approach to the giving of the Exercises was very flexible, and always focused on the needs of the individual retreatant.

As with all the retreats considered in this book, the Exercises are given without any consideration of denomination. Their popularity today extends right across – and beyond – the spectrum of the various Christian traditions.

In a shorter **individually given retreat** in the Ignatian tradition, (usually the traditional six- or eight-day retreat), the process is less rigorous, much more individually tailored to where you feel you are when you come on retreat. You will probably not be aware that you are 'doing the Exercises' in any obvious way, but it is likely that the journey of prayer that you make with your guide alongside will be picking up something of the dynamic of the Exercises as it seems to apply to your present situation. It is important to understand that an eight-day Ignatian retreat is not meant to be a condensed 'mini' version of the Exercises, but an experience of prayer that is nourished by the dynamic of the Exercises as appropriate to you at that time.

The cost of making the full Exercises in a retreat centre amounts to the cost of accommodation and spiritual direction for 30 to 36 days. There are several centres offering the full Exercises, some with full board (which are obviously more expensive) and some on a self-catering basis. On current (2002) prices, you might be looking at a budget of about £45 per 24-hour period, for full-board accommodation, and rather less if you are self-catering.

If you apply to make the full Exercises in the seclusion of a retreat centre you may find that the organizers will ask for references, and reserve the right to reject your application. This is because the process is a demanding one, both physically, emotionally and spiritually, and the retreat centre needs to have some assurance that you will be able to cope with the demands of such intensive prayer within an environment of near-total silence. It would in any case be unwise to enter into the process of the full Exercises without having first made a few shorter silent individually given retreats, and without having had the experience of ongoing spiritual direction (or '**soul friendship**') in daily life.

Having said that, to make the full Exercises of St Ignatius is frequently a life-changing and deeply rewarding experience.

Spirituality networks

During the last few years the general understanding of the word 'spirituality' has moved from being something utterly esoteric, and the domain of monks, nuns and hermits, to a concept that many people, both inside and beyond the visible 'church' can and do relate to. There is no doubt that a hunger for meaning in life and a serious quest for an experience of the authentic mystery at the core of our being is rapidly increasing and spreading. Sadly, there is also a growing awareness that organized religion, in its traditional forms, seems to be able to do little to satisfy this hunger or facilitate this quest.

One of the ways in which people are beginning to get in touch with the spiritual dimension of their being is through the growing availability of retreats and quiet days, especially those that can be undertaken in daily life. Many people come away from an experience of retreat with a sharpened appetite for the search for God's presence and direction in their living. In time such people gravitate together and form local networks. Some of these are totally informal. Others are highly organized. All could be described under the umbrella term of 'spirituality network'.

A spirituality network tends to evolve for the following reasons:

- As a support network for people in a particular locality who are engaged in the giving of retreats to others or have a personal interest in developing their own spiritual lives and sharing their exploration with others. A local network will often facilitate retreats and quiet days for its members, and will usually organize plenary gatherings at regular intervals. The larger networks occasionally also organize conferences.
- As an information base, enabling anyone seeking spiritual companionship to contact someone who lives in their neighbourhood. Some local networks hold an impressive database of contact names, including details of any particular expertise, extent of training, or special interests of the individuals. If you are moving house, for example, and hoping to find contact with people in the new locality who are spiritually 'on your wavelength', you might do well to make a start by contacting a local spirituality network.

Spirituality networks will normally be:

- Ecumenical;
- Open equally to lay and ordained people;
- Independent of the structures of any of the institutional churches;
- Non profit-making.

They will make you welcome whether you have any contact with a Christian church or not.

The cost of membership of a spirituality network varies considerably, depending on the facilities it offers. If the network maintains a database of contact names and addresses, there will be a nominal charge to have your name included, and to receive a copy of the register, which also needs regular updating. Some networks produce a regular newsletter, advertising forthcoming retreats and quiet days, and often including articles on topics of general interest or aspects of spirituality.

The Retreat Association holds information on at least some of the networks that have evolved around the UK. (See Contact Addresses at the end of this book.)

Supervision

Whatever form of retreat you make, whether in daily life or in a retreat house, over a day or over 30 days, your **retreat guide** will have a supervisor.

The purpose of supervision is to provide a space where those engaged in accompanying others can open up any issues that are arising for them in their own journeying. When listening to the issues of other people, it can very easily happen that something is said that touches a sensitive nerve in the companion. A good guide will never reveal to the retreatant that this has happened, but may need to speak to someone about what has been touched upon.

It must be emphasized that supervision never entails revealing anything at all about those being accompanied, or about anything that was said during the one-to-one meetings. Ideally the supervisor will not know who the guide is accompanying, and will be from a different area or parish, with no personal contact with any of the retreatants. Whether this is the case or not, the guide has a responsibility to conceal the identity of everyone he or she is accompanying, when in supervision. The material for supervision is strictly the guide's own journey and any issues that may have come up in that connection.

If the guide does need practical help and guidance in helping a retreatant, that help will be sought with utmost discretion, changing all the details if necessary, so as to protect the confidentiality of the retreatant.

From the retreatant's point of view, the fact of supervision provides a safeguard. It means that a third person is present to the retreat and will not hesitate to warn the guide if he or she appears to be allowing a personal agenda to be activated by what the retreatant is sharing. This agenda can then be taken, as it were, 'off-line' and dealt with in supervision, so that it is less likely to impact the dialogue with the retreatant.

Supervision has been described as a place where retreat guides can open up doors that have so far been closed in their own journeying. A retreatant may inadvertently 'knock on' one of those closed doors, and the guide notices an inner reaction to that 'knock'. Perhaps something has been mentioned that the guide herself is trying to avoid looking at in her own life. When this happens, guides are trained to observe their own reactions and take what they find into supervision.

Anyone who is offering ongoing '**soul friendship**' or 'spiritual direction' will likewise have both a supervisor and a 'soul friend' or 'spiritual director' of their own. No one can give to others what they are not receiving themselves, in the field of spiritual companionship.

Theme retreats

Especially for people coming new to the idea of making a retreat, a 'theme retreat' might be a gentler approach to taking time apart in stillness and reflection than plunging straight into the experience of being individually guided.

A theme retreat may be focused on almost any topic. A glance through *Retreats* or through the church press will reveal something of the variety of topics available. The experience of a theme retreat is in some ways less intensive than that of an **individually given retreat**. Though there may be periods of silence, these will be interleaved with periods of listening to the speaker or retreat leader, possibly sharing your reflections with a small group of the other retreatants, and meeting together in open forum to raise any questions or make any comments.

You will have already selected a theme that interests you, and you will be approaching the retreat in the hope of deepening your insights on the topic concerned, or exploring more deeply the issue under discussion. This will then become the focus of your prayer during the time of the retreat. The retreat leader may have prepared handouts summarizing the themes to be covered, and may well suggest a particular way of focusing your prayer during the quiet time. You must, of course, follow the promptings of the Holy Spirit in your prayer, wherever they lead, and anything the retreat leader gives you is only intended as a suggestion, or as a guide to those who are not sure where to begin their prayer.

Some theme retreats will include tuition or help in a particular skill, such as painting or calligraphy, as well as providing a spiritual focus for the activity concerned. This will usually be clear from the description of the retreat either in *Retreats* or in the publicity material provided by the retreat house. If you are in any doubt, ask the retreat house for full details of what help is available.

A theme retreat can last for anything from a day to ten days or more, but the average duration probably lies around four or five days, if the retreat is being offered in a retreat house. The cost is equivalent to that of an individually given retreat, amounting to the cost of accommodation and full board (if applicable) and the costs incurred by the speaker. On current rates (2002), you would need to budget for about £45 per 24-hour period for a retreat including full board, and rather less if you are catering for yourself. The retreat house will give you full details of cost on request, and in many cases early booking is advisable.

The structure of the days depends, of course, entirely upon the retreat leader and the director of the retreat house. An example of how a day might run is indicated under the heading '**Daily routine on retreat**'.

In a theme retreat lasting for several days, it is likely that the retreat leader will also be available for one-to-one conversations if you wish.

PART V

Retreatants Speak for Themselves

In this section people who have made a variety of different types of retreat share a first-hand account of their experience.

Keeping Mum before God

Life as a mother of two small children is always wonderful, but it can be exhausting. There are times, too, especially when the children are very small and at home full-time, that Mum's very identity (the one before 'Mum'!) seems to disappear beneath the nappies, storybooks and duplo bricks. We wouldn't be human if we didn't sometimes cry 'there must be more to life than this'. So when a friend asked me to join a retreat at a retreat house in Kent, I didn't hesitate. My enormously supportive husband can manage perfectly well without me and pushed me out of the house with instructions to rest and enjoy.

A retreat can be restful, but it can also provide refreshment through challenge and it wasn't an easy weekend. Going from the busyness of family life to retreat (especially a silent one, as this was) was a challenge. It was wonderful to eat a lovely meal without having to cook or wash up, but it took a while to let go and it was helpful to have someone to direct the retreat and to move my thoughts away from the mundane.

The countryside around the retreat house is lovely and I enjoyed being able to walk at grown-up pace and in silence. It is situated near Brands Hatch and the sound of speeding motors prompted me to pray for the world I'd retreated from. In the absence of the constant voice of the toddler, I found myself surprised – even disturbed – by God. I told him that I wanted more out of life. Gracious and merciful, he even let me shout at him (yes, I did shout, even though it was a silent retreat!). I was well out of earshot and felt thoroughly released by it; with that out of my system, it was easier for me to listen to God. At the end of the lovely garden is a cross; there God spoke to me.

I thought I needed something new, something that would restore 'my' identity. Instead, God challenged and strengthened me to persevere with the task in hand. The retreat helped me to live in the now and not in the 'I wish'; it also allowed God to be a parent to me. By the end I was aching to get back to my daughters and husband, to get back to the task that really is 'me'. So, on a sunny Sunday afternoon, I drove home to my family, ready to go on with the best job in the world – being Mum.

Beverley Hollins (reproduced with permission from *Retreats*, 2000)

Six weeks that made a difference

I was thrilled at first, when the prospect of a retreat was mentioned at the faith sharing group I belonged to. I had always wanted to make a retreat for as long as I knew that such things happened. I didn't really have much of an idea what it would entail, but I knew it was something I wanted to do.

I remember arriving home that night and telling the family my news. 'There's going to be a retreat,' I said. 'I hope there's no objection to me taking part.'

I could see from their faces that they were underimpressed.

'What's a retreat, when it's at home?' my teenage son muttered, rather sullenly from the depths of his pile of homework.

'Mummy, you're not going away are you?' my younger daughter cried, with panic in her voice.

My husband just looked at me over the top of the newspaper. 'Another fad,' I thought I heard him thinking, 'She'll get over it.'

But maybe that's being unfair to him. At all events, nobody could come up with any real reason why I shouldn't take part, so the following week I registered for the daily life retreat, relieved to have got over this first hurdle.

The time arrived for the opening meeting. A dozen or so of us gathered in the church hall. By this time the reality of the venture was beginning to dawn on me. Suppose I made a huge mess of it! Suppose I didn't know what to say to my companion! Suppose I just couldn't pray! All of a sudden, my enthusiasm turned to panic, and I nearly backed right out.

But the retreat leader seemed to have the knack of dispelling our fears. He led us very gently into a time of stillness, helping us to experience practical ways of relaxing, and sinking down to the deeper parts of ourselves. Then he explained how the retreat would work, how we would meet our companions once a week, and what those meetings would be like. Then came the crunch. We were allocated to our prayer companions. I glanced at the four 'companions' who were sitting in the circle with us. Which one would I choose? Which one would I least want? The panic was rising again.

I needn't have worried. Barbara smiled across at me, as my name was read out, and we went out together, with her other three retreatants, to arrange times to meet, and to get to know each other a little. Perhaps, I thought, it wouldn't be so impossible to share something of my prayer with her.

And so to the first meeting. Barbara had already given me a scripture passage to use as a focus for prayer. And I really had tried to make time for prayer each day. Sometimes I managed the silent 15 minutes I had promised myself. Once I totally failed. And one day I had to cut the time short, when my daughter came bursting in to tell me that the cat had been sick. I could only hope that God – and Barbara – would be forgiving!

But there was never any question of reproach, when things went awry. I never once had the feeling that Barbara was judging me in any way. She just listened, and while I was with her, I got the feeling that I was the only person in her life. She gave me her undivided attention, and somehow that helped me, too, to attend wholeheartedly to what God had been doing in my life during the days between our meetings.

Soon, the time with God each day became something I looked forward to. It gave me real nourishment and a base-line of inner peace that carried me through the rest of the day. I found that I wanted to pray more, and perhaps differently, and Barbara introduced me to ways of praying with scripture that I'd never known about before.

Those six weeks were a major turning point in my life. Perhaps that was when my journey with God moved beyond 'religion' into 'relationship'. When the children are a bit older I hope to go away on a residential retreat one year. Meanwhile I will certainly be joining in the next daily life retreat. And there will be another one. All of us who made the retreat are determined to make sure of that!

Ann Ashton

'Hands-on' Lenten retreat

It was a great relief, when our artist retreat leader said we had to come with an empty mind. My mind was completely empty – I was not arty – I had no craft skills. I was not sure why I was there to pray the passion and cross of Jesus in paint, clay, sculptural relief and mixed media.

'Let's start by making a cross out of newspaper' said our leader. I couldn't believe my response – I did not want to make a cross – I could not make a cross – I felt like a stubborn child. I needed to reflect on this.

Crosses were painful, destructive, agonizing experiences, not to be trivialized. I couldn't make a cross of newspaper. I had come to the retreat to know God more, so I thought a ladder to climb up to him might be more appropriate – so I made a paper ladder. But no, that was not right. God was a presence within me, not up there, so with some force and satisfaction, I crunched the ladder into a ball.

Then I found myself adding layers of newspaper and coloured paper round this ball. Were these the layers of myself, which had to be removed in order to know more of this mystery called God? I knew there were parts of me that sometimes held me back from reaching out to others. I wanted to cross this gulf and give myself freely.

I soon had a crumpled paper ball a little smaller than a football. It needed to be held together, so I stuck on two lengths of white tape – only to see, to my surprise, that I had made a cross. I still did not want a cross, so I placed two more pieces of tape and felt that the ball/me was now held together in the security of love.

I reflected on the paper ball overnight. I thought of the time of my own crucifixion – a time of anguish, or a nightmare quality. This had lasted a long time, yet my faith in a positive outcome was never in doubt and in the end I was strengthened in my certainty of God's presence in all that happens to us. But it did not feel like that at the time!

So now I wished that I had placed a cross at the centre of my ball.

The next morning I talked to our artist prayer companion and we agreed to open the ball – see what was inside and place a cross there. It was difficult to cut through the screwed up paper but I managed it, made a little wooden cross and covered it in gold paper. The cross was an essential part of me, which had given me the experience of the compassion and glory of love.

Now what to do with the falling-apart two halves of the ball, now only lightly joined at the base?

Some stronger pieces to hold it together as I was held during my ordeal?

Again, quiet reflection in the chapel, holding my crumpled ball with the golden cross secure in the middle. Then the true nature of crucifixion – Jesus' and mine – came to me. It was a falling apart, a disintegration, a losing of all that had meaning, all security. Could I allow my own ball creation to remain fragile and vulnerable? More reflection, then I knew the only honest thing to do was to leave it without support, to accept the possibility of its fragmentation. Disintegration, fragmentation, words and experiences to be avoided, but I was not distressed. I knew that through these experiences it was possible to be held together and renewed. By what? That is the Mystery!

Dorothy Millichamp

Paint and clay – A passion retreat

I approached Easter with some apprehension: I have never found it an easy season but this year was special. I had signed up for a retreat in daily life, 'Praying the passion and cross of Jesus in paint, clay, sculptural relief and mixed media.' It was to be held in our church over four days, beginning with a plenary meeting at Sunday teatime.

Around 30 people, from various churches, gathered to meet the leaders – a priest and a visual artist and sculptor – and to explore the abundance of creative materials available. After the first evening there was a choice of sessions each day.

We began with the Eucharist, which included an impromptu dramatic reading of the passion story. Afterwards we were free to 'pray the passion' in our own way and in our own time. I didn't know where to begin, so I resorted to what was familiar to me, a lump of clay. During the service I had been 'bugged' by some lines from an ancient hymn 'deep in thy wounds Lord, hide and shelter me', and 'wash me with the water, flowing from thy side'. I picked up my clay and squeezed it hard and put a slash in its side. I then made a tiny figure and tried to put it in the gash. It was too big! Food for thought; either I had to become smaller or Jesus had to become bigger – the clay had already become Jesus and me! Gradually I found myself adding and shaping the original lump to form a recognizable torso and I was being protected by a loving arm. It felt OK.

I had been struck by the attitudes of the various people in the passion story and wanted to explore this. During my sleep that night I dreamed I saw hands and arms in all sorts of gestures, and the next morning I spotted an advertisement depicting similar positions. I photocopied these and enlarged them as I knew that they were significant, but wasn't sure how to use them. The artist who was, like the priest, always at hand to offer help if needed, scattered the pages on the floor and they fell roughly into the shape of a cross. I'd had no intention of depicting anything so obvious as a cross! However the rhythm of the stylized gestures made it a very powerful statement of authority and condemnation which could not be ignored. Colin, the artist, asked me if I knew I could photocopy my hands. I experimented with various gestures and was intrigued by what emerged – the shadows, the lights, the hints and suggestions of form or substance, and the blackness, always the blackness.

These were my hands, and I put them in the form of a cross. This made a strong impact. These were my hands, my hidden agendas – it wasn't so much about what I'd actually said or done, it was my inner attitudes – even my 'open' palm was half hidden; I too was one of Christ's accusers. Whew!

Then I looked at my first creation – I had almost come full circle. I recognized my need to be washed and sheltered deep in his wounds. I didn't want to do a cross, I didn't want to think about it; and yet I was drawn there, that's where my focus was. There was light, even in the darkness of the cross; there was hope; there was life in looking.

This was a very intensive few days. Even though I was living at home, with all the domestic tasks this entails, it was part of a whole. There were no separate prayer times as such: kneading clay, photocopying, preparing meals, clearing up, reflecting, sharing with God my thoughts and feelings – all were interwoven as prayer.

Mary Griffiths

A reluctant retreatant remembers . . .

I am now a widow, with two grown-up sons, and for years I had been thinking about going on a retreat, but never actually done so. Then last year, for various reasons, I began to ask more questions, realizing that all my previous excuses for not going on retreat were rapidly becoming irrelevant. Eventually I heard about a weekend retreat planned to take place not too far from where I live. I asked several close friends for advice. Their response ranged from 'Go! It will do you good' to 'You already spend a lot of time on your own. Why would you want to spend two days in silence among strangers?' One friend summed it up: 'Why not go? It's only for two days if you find you hate it, but you'll never know until you try.' So I decided to go for it. A Christian friend offered to accompany me and to drive us there. So I booked.

Before I went I was very nervous indeed, and almost convinced myself that I was making a terrible mistake. But as soon as we arrived, we were made really welcome. I was shown to simple but pleasant room overlooking the garden. Soon afterwards my friend came along to invite me to go to the service of vespers in the chapel – a service I had never attended before in my life. Again, my instinct was to say 'No', but then I thought 'Why not?', went along with her, and to my surprise felt much calmer afterwards. The evening arrived, and we went to the first of the talks given by the retreat leader, after which the silence began. By then I was already beginning to enjoy the weekend.

Normally I have difficulty in getting up in the morning, but that night I slept very well, and woke early the next morning. The retreat centre was so peaceful. It seemed a shame just to stay in bed. I got dressed and went, instead, to the lauds service in the chapel before breakfast.

Another talk followed on Saturday morning, but Saturday afternoon was left completely free. About three and a half hours of free time, in silence, was quite a daunting prospect for me, and it was, perhaps, the most challenging part of the retreat. I spent most of the time in the garden, enjoying the short summer heatwave, and was ready for the third talk in the evening. I ended the day by sharing in the compline service in the chapel before all the retreatants joined with the retreat leader for a period of evening prayer together. It seemed right to start and end the day with God like this.

On the Sunday I again chose to go to lauds before breakfast, and then we all shared in the Eucharist, which was beautiful. The final talk followed, before lunch, and in the afternoon we slipped back into quiet talking before leaving for home.

Before I went I had been really fearful of the expected silence from Friday evening to Sunday afternoon, but in the event I found it calming, peaceful and friendly and not at all oppressive. Before I booked I had wondered to myself: 'What do you take into a retreat? What do you take away from it?' Now I know the answers. I took into that retreat someone who was tired, tense and nervous. When I left (reluctantly) two days later, I brought away someone who was calmer, happier, refreshed, and more sure of my faith. A very good result! What I had feared was going to be difficult turned out to be gold – God's gold! I would recommend it to anyone.

Kerry Hiscock

A Birmingham solicitor on retreat in working life

I was given details about the retreat in daily life by a colleague. My immediate thoughts were to dismiss the idea of attending because I felt there was a conflict between the concept of a retreat and my less than restful and quiet daily life as a wife, mother and solicitor. In the weeks between receiving the information and the start of the retreat, God impressed on my mind the need to learn to quieten myself and find stillness in his presence each day and so I decided to attend although I remained apprehensive.

The retreat was structured over a six-week period. It commenced with an introductory meeting which was attended by all pilgrims and prayer guides. The closing evening was also attended by all pilgrims and prayer guides and provided an opportunity to share our retreat experiences, both positive and negative, and to pray together. In the intervening weeks arrangements were made between the pilgrim and prayer guide to meet each week for about half an hour, at a time and place convenient to both. I met my prayer guide each Friday at 8.15 a.m. in Birmingham Cathedral, and on each occasion we found a quiet corner to talk and pray without disturbing others or being disturbed, except on our last meeting when the organist had an early practice!

During the first week I prayed imaginatively from scripture and was amazed at the way God spoke to me directly about every part of my life – home, work and church. In the following weeks I prayed meditatively from scripture and again God spoke to me in the stillness about all aspects of my life and matters which were currently troubling me, as well as certain traumatic events in the past.

I was helped enormously by my prayer guide who was a wise, discerning, godly woman with the gift of listening. At our weekly meetings to discuss my prayer journey she led me to passages of scripture to pray over – sometimes a short psalm, sometimes a longer passage – to enable me to continue my journey. She simply listened and only offered advice when I asked for it. The passages of scripture she suggested were always relevant and helpful. I felt that the way she listened and gently suggested the next step reflected the gentle and loving way God was leading me in my prayer journey.

I was only able to devote about ten minutes each day to pray, yet God honoured that commitment and I was amazed how God spoke during these short periods of stillness and quiet.

During the retreat I began to feel in my heart truths which I had carried in my head for many years. I learned that God is with me in every part of my life, that I must trust him at all times, and my understanding of my circumstances should not affect my trust in God's good and perfect purpose for every part of my life. I found the retreat one of the most spiritually significant things I have done in recent years and I feel that it has given me the tools with which to continue to build a deeper relationship with God each day, and integrate the different spheres of my life.

Deborah Oram

Two pilgrims make the Spiritual Exercises of St Ignatius in daily life

Several years ago, after completing an intensive ecumenical two-year course on prayer, I found myself desiring prayer in an even deeper way, a hunger to listen and hear God, for the needs of my own church as minister for prayer, as well as a desire to seek God's will for my own life.

What other attractions did the idea of praying with St Ignatius hold for me? I could see two immediately: the idea of 'overcoming self' – it had always seemed to me that only 'holy' people had the key to this – and the attraction of a life based on making decisions in complete freedom from attachments. After praying about it, I decided to go ahead.

One significant warm and bright September day my spiritual director arrived at the door. She was a Roman Catholic nun who gently took me through the Exercises. They were to last until Eastertime the following year. I found the ordered and structured way of prayer suited me well, and it was to give me the freedom in prayer that I was seeking.

After accepting and understanding the principle and foundation, that it is God who creates all our qualities, insights, patience, talents, as well as our freedom; that God is the ground of all being; and asking God for grace that all my actions might be directed to God's praise and service, I was ready to move on.

My director asked me to spend an hour in prayer each day. As a Reader in the Anglican Church I had sermons to prepare, and worship leading to plan and reflect on, as well as other church and family activities. However, once I had made my commitment to prayer I found myself wanting to increase the time I spent with God.

The first stage of the Exercises journey delved to a deeper knowledge and understanding of personal sinfulness, weaknesses and limitations. This led me on to reflect deeply on the misery of the world. From feelings of desolation came profound joy that in Jesus Christ is true healing. As each stage of the Exercises was completed, there came a clarity of vision and openness to the Spirit. This was affirmation of my faith.

After listening, discerning and responding, I accepted God's call to me to a deeper commitment within the church.

In no time at all, Easter came. The final two stages of the Exercises, Christ's passion, death and resurrection, left me with an experience of deep sorrow, as I shared in his sufferings, which stirred within a greater desire to serve and live for God. A desire to live a life grounded in God – pleasing God and enacting the desires he creates in the deepness of self. I found myself with a deeper wisdom about pain and suffering which, little as I could have known it at the time, would be such a blessing to me later on in my own circumstances, as well as an empathy with others' pain. This was followed by the joy of resurrection.

There was a postscript to my Exercises journey, reminding me that we do find God in all things: Holidaying in Cyprus some months later, I was walking high in the mountains with my husband. The terrain became more rocky and barren. I exclaimed, 'This must be similar to Jesus in the wilderness.' There appeared to be no living thing, except ourselves, until I spotted the most beautiful bright blue flower, nodding in the wind. It was breathtakingly alive, in the barrenness. How could it survive? How did it get there? Did the wind carry it? Having just completed the Spiritual Exercises, I heard it speak volumes to me, and I believe God had especially put it there to speak to me. It assured me that I would survive, no matter how rough the going might get, whatever circumstances might overtake me.

Now I accompany others in prayer myself, and discover how wonderful it is to share the journey of the heart with each other – just one way of trying to learn to love as God loves.

Rosemary Millward

The Nineteenth Annotation

My decision to undertake the Nineteenth Annotation retreat was not taken lightly. It followed quite a long period of deepening personal prayer, a week's silent retreat and a growing awareness of a deep-seated dis-ease deep within my being. I chose to make my retreat on a one-to-one basis rather than in a group as I knew instinctively that the direction of personal discovery was not something I would be able to share in a group situation.

I entered my retreat knowing that I was searching for acceptance, freedom and a deep sense of being loved. I was told that the retreat would change my life, but nothing had prepared me for the way in which this would happen. The impact on my life was profound, it turned it upside down! I found my initial desires of love, and of freedom from fear of being myself were fulfilled. It deepened my heart's desire for depths of loving and giving that I had previously only dreamed of. However, light casts shadows, and it was during this retreat that the shadow side of my being was revealed, the serious nature of my own propensity for sin, my attachment to my own self-esteem and other facets of my personality were illuminated.

On reflection I feel that the real impact of this retreat occurred quite a few weeks after the retreat itself had ended. Even three years later I am still aware of this impact; it echoes in my life, comforting, highlighting potential dangers.

In many ways I found the prayer experiences of the first week were actually quite prophetic in that personal weaknesses were exposed and the darkness of sin assumed a clarity never before experienced.

The middle weeks of the retreat revealed a very vulnerable Saviour whose humanity was tangible. Here I found Jesus, a man to love and one who loved me with an intensity that still leaves me in awe of its depth and beauty. These weeks taught me the meaning of 'loved sinner', they taught me to be unafraid of my own feelings and emotions, and that life was experienced and expressed through these same emotions. I became alive and happy, renewed in every sense of the word.

The process of discernment was a journey of discovery too. Life is not black and white, and the variations of shades of grey make discernment difficult. I have learned to take much more care in interpreting my prayer images, as misinterpretation leads into rough seas.

Overall I found this retreat one of the most positive and enjoyable experiences in my life. The Nineteenth Annotation in daily life spans a nine-month period, a long time to commit to, but the focus it gives to prayer and the dynamic it has on life makes it all worthwhile. I also found for me the timespan was beneficial, allowing the changes experienced to be more fully assimilated into life, which for me was vitally important as I needed my prayer to be firmly grounded in life.

I would like to make this retreat again one day, as a 30-day retreat to consolidate the changes experienced and to renew again an openness of spirit in a period of time specifically and specially set aside for prayer.

Teresa Booth

An experience of a 30-day retreat

Have you ever asked yourself the questions, 'Who am I now?', Where am I going?', and 'Where is God in my life at this moment?' These were some of the questions that were around for me a few years ago when I was faced with major changes in direction in my life. It was at this time that I made the 30-day retreat – the Exercises of St Ignatius.

To be able to spend a month away from the busyness of my life and ministry and to have time to look again at what my call to conversion was about seemed scary and challenging, yet inviting. The Exercises have their own dynamic and rhythm, and these reflections and meditations alongside selected scripture passages gave me the space to begin to discover what real freedom was about. In the beginning I began to rediscover the power and the presence of God in all of creation. There was so much I had begun to take for granted mainly because of my involvement in ministry and in the notion of 'doing things for God'. I had time to appreciate what was around me and how everything comes from God and is for God's glory. This in turn put me in touch with my own vulnerability and weakness at times but I was constantly amazed at how God was ever compassionate and loving – always ready to forgive and to go on loving me.

As I moved further into the Exercises I began to discover those things in my life which contribute to a lack of freedom in the way I was living. The Exercises at this stage helped me to a deeper awareness as to the choices I make and the ultimate meaning of life. I was on this journey with Jesus sharing in his life and ministry while being made more aware of what it really means to choose Jesus as my leader. I found myself being challenged to accept who I was as God saw me. This brought a great freedom, a sense of true identity and a basic peace in my life. I was drawn more and more to the depths within me and to find a place of peace and love within. This was not always a time of peace and I experienced moments of struggle and conflict when what I felt called to do differed from what God was inviting me to.

There were times of emptiness and confusion too, but ultimately the call to conversion was strongest and the unfailing love of God for me, was always my source of strength. I found God right in the centre of the mess and the chaos as well as in the more serene and peaceful moments. As the Exercises progressed, the process of discernment in the Exercises of St Ignatius helped me towards clarity and vision but it was now based on a deeper, inner conversion, and I could see that whatever I did would flow from that depth of God within me. This retreat was about finding God in everything and this raised many challenges for me around issues of justice in the world.

This long retreat is all about God's call and the way we respond to it. It is something that has to be lived every day and so the Exercises have become, for me, a way of life. Living them in the busy world of ministry is often very different to the 30 days I spent 'on the mountain', but God is the same and it is God's constant invitation to freedom and energy that has made my life so much more meaningful and alive. It's a day-to-day choice for me and it's about remaining centred and focused on the things that are important. The 30-day retreat helped me to rediscover the dream God has for me.

Breda Gainey SSJA

Contact addresses

When approaching any of the contacts listed below to request written information, please enclose a stamped, addressed envelope.

The Retreat Association
The Central Hall
256 Bermondsey Street
London SE1 3UJ
Tel: 020 7357 7736
Fax: 020 7357 7724
e-mail: info@retreats.org.uk
Internet: http://www.retreats.org.uk

Association for Promoting Retreats
Contact Membership Secretary at the Retreat Association office (address above)

Baptist Union Retreat Group
Contact:
Pamela Neville
42 Coniston Road
Chippenham
Wiltshire SN14 0PX

Methodist Retreat and Spirituality Network
Contact:
Edward Smith
7 Waterthorpe Glade
Westfield
Sheffield S20 8LX

National Retreat Movement
Contact Membership Secretary at the Retreat Association Office (see address above)

Quaker Retreat Group
Flat 30 Anthony Road
Wroughton
Swindon SN4 9HN

United Reformed Church Silence and Retreats Network
Contact:
Revd David Bunney
19 Abbey Road
Sudbury
Suffolk CO10 1LA

Christian Life Community
St Joseph's
Watford Way
London NW4 4TY

The Julian Meetings
Contact:
Mrs Anne Stamper
The Firs
Lewes Road
Ringmer
Lewes
East Sussex BN8 SEU

The Quiet Garden Trust
Stoke Park Farm
Park Road
Stoke Poges
Bucks SL2 4PG

A number of local spirituality networks exist throughout the United Kingdom, to promote Christian spirituality and support those engaged in spiritual direction and guided prayer. For details of a network local to your area, please ask for the most up-to-date details from the Retreat Association.

Some suggestions for further reading

Prayer and personality

Bruce Duncan, *Pray your Way: Your Personality and God*, Darton, Longman and Todd, 1994 (an introduction to Myers Briggs).

Dr Charles J. Keating, *Who We Are Is How We Pray: Matching Personality and Spirituality*, Twenty-Third Publications, 1987 (also based on Myers Briggs).

Angela Reith, *Who Am I?: Discovering Your Personality with the Enneagram*, Lion Publishing (Giftlines), 1999.

Don Richard Riso, *Personality Types: Using the Enneagram for Self-Discovery*, Aquarian, 1987.

The spiritual journey

Francis Dewar, *Live for a Change*, Darton, Longman and Todd (2nd edition) 1999.

Margaret Guenther, *Holy Listening: The Art of Spiritual Direction*, Darton, Longman and Todd, 1992.

Gerard W. Hughes, *God of Surprises*, Darton, Longman and Todd, 1985 (also available as a group package with accompanying cassette).

Kenneth Leech, *Soul Friend: Spiritual Direction in the Modern World*, Darton, Longman and Todd, 1994.

David Londsdale SJ, *Dance to the Music of the Spirit: The Art of Discernment*, Darton, Longman and Todd, 1992.

Margaret Silf, *Landmarks: An Ignatian Journey* and *Wayfaring: A Gospel Journey into Life*, Darton, Longman and Todd, 1998 and 2001.

Ray Simpson, *Soul Friendship: Celtic Insights Into Spiritual Mentoring*, Hodder and Stoughton, 1999.

Prayer

William A. Barry SJ, *God and You: Prayer as Personal Relationship*, Paulist Press, 1987.

William A. Barry SJ, *What Do I Want in Prayer?*, Paulist Press, 1994.

Catherine de Hueck Doherty, *Poustinia: Encountering God in Silence*, Solitude and Prayer, Madonna House Publishing, 2000.

Meryl Doney, *The Art of Prayer: A Pathway to Spiritual Growth*, Lion Publishing (Giftlines), 1999.

Monica Furlong, *Contemplating Now*, Cowley Publications, 1971.

Thomas H. Green SJ, *Opening to God: A Guide to Prayer*, Ave Maria Press, 1977.

Kenneth Leech, *True Prayer: An Introduction to Christian Spirituality*, Sheldon Press, 1980.

Dennis Linn, Sheila Fabricant Linn, Matthew Linn, *Sleeping with Bread: Holding What Gives You Life*, Paulist Press, 1995.

Anthony de Mello, *Awareness*, Fount Paperbacks, 1990.

Margaret Silf, *Taste and See: Adventuring Into Prayer*, Darton, Longman and Todd, 1999.

Retreats

Thomas Hart, *Coming down the Mountain: How to Turn Your Retreat Into Everyday Living*, Paulist Press, 1988.

Andrew Nash, *Making a Retreat*, Methodist Retreat Group, 2000.

Gillian Russell, *Finding the Right Retreat for You*, Hunt and Thorpe, 1994.

Stafford Whiteaker, *The Good Retreat Guide*, Rider Books.

Making a self-directed retreat

Thomas H. Green SJ, *A Vacation with the Lord: A Personal Directed Retreat*, Ave Maria Press, 1986.

Brother Ramon SSF, *Seven Days of Solitude: A Guidebook for a Personal Retreat*, Hodder and Stoughton, 2000.

Margaret Silf, *Sacred Spaces: Stations on a Celtic Way*, Lion Publishing, 2001 (material suitable for a seven- or eight-day self-directed retreat in the tradition of Celtic spirituality).

There are also several helpful series of books that may be useful, including:

The *Praying with ...* series in *Companions for the Journey*, published by St Mary's Press, Minnesota. The series includes volumes on praying with most of the spiritual giants in the Christian tradition.

The *A Retreat with ...* series, published by St Antony's Messenger Press, Ohio. Each volume in this series provides material for a self-directed retreat with two spiritual giants in dialogue together. The reader is invited to engage with this dialogue.

The *Fifteen Days of Prayer with ...* series, published by Liguori, Missouri. Each book in the series contains a biography of a seminal spiritual figure, a guide for setting up a format of prayer and retreat, and material for 15 prayer periods.

Index

Ignatian networks 7, 125
Ignatius Loyola 7, 125
IGR 16, 106
Individually given/guided retreats
    16, 106
Internet 8
Introspection, value of 37
Introverts, in solitude 48

Jesuits 125
Journalling 92
Julian meetings 7, 108

Lay people
    as guides/companions 42, 112
    as retreatants 42
Leaving retreat 20, 32
    prematurely 49
Life choices, discernment of 31,
    128
'Long retreat' 31
Low cost retreats 61

Marriage preparation retreats 34
MBTI® 109
Myers Briggs Typology
    Indicator® 109

Nineteenth Annotation retreats 6,
    122
Non-practising Christians 43

Ongoing spiritual companionship
    6, 120
'Open Door retreats' 4, 110
Opposition from family 40
Other faiths 43

Pacing 86
Parish retreats/weekends 25
Pilgrimage 30

Place for prayer, finding 78
Prayer companion/Prayer guide
    53, 112
Prayer exercises 19
Preached retreats 24, 42
Preparation for retreat
    personal 78
    practical 75
Prison retreats 5
Problem solving 27, 103

Quiet days 10, 113
Quiet gardens 12, 114

Reading during retreat 50, 67, 77
Recreation 67, 82
Reflection on prayer 84
Reflective living 84, 90
Relationship counselling 41
Religious vocations, discernment
    of 33
Resolutions 93
Rest days 32
Retreat Association xiii, 94
Retreat centre, choice of 21
Retreat guide/director 19, 39, 106,
    115
    conversations with 55, 58
    daily meeting with 19, 86, 106
    expectations of 56
    relationship with 59
'Retreats Beyond Dover' 29
Retreats in daily life 3, 41, 118
Retreats magazine xiv, 95
Retreats on the streets 12
Returning home 20, 32

Same sex couples 41, 53
Scripture 46
Self-catering retreats 21
Self-directed retreats 9

161